C0-ASP-779

THE SENSUOUS CHRISTIAN

THE

SENSUOUS CHRISTIAN

A Celebration of Freedom and Love

LAWRENCE MEREDITH

ASSOCIATION PRESS
NEW YORK

2 0915
M 541

185712

THE SENSUOUS CHRISTIAN

Copyright © 1972 by Lawrence Meredith

Association Press, 291 Broadway, New York, N.Y. 10007

All rights reserved. No part of this publication may be reprinted,
reproduced, transmitted, stored in a retrieval system, or otherwise
utilized, in any form or by any means, electronic or mechanical,
including photocopying or recording, now existing or hereinafter
invented, without the prior written permission of the publisher.

International Standard Book Number: 0-8096-1852-4
Library of Congress Catalog Card Number: 72-8225

Library of Congress Cataloging in Publication Data
Meredith, Lawrence, 1928–
    Sensuous Christian.

    Includes bibliographical references.
    1. Christianity—20th century. 2. Theology—20th
century. I. Title.
BR121.2.M42   209'.04   72-8225
ISBN 0-8096-1852-4

PRINTED IN THE UNITED STATES OF AMERICA

To my sensuous wife

Admittedly, for the majority of young people today, the Western tradition is quite dead. . . . Chaplains neither can revive it nor, in my opinion, do they *have* any doctrine to teach. But they can provide centers, and be centers, for confusion to express itself.

—PAUL GOODMAN, Introduction to
Never Trust a God Over Thirty

The sources for insight and information throughout this book are often cited, and I owe much more than can be documented anywhere. Still I must lift up thanks to some special people here: to Betty Beckler for being (and typing), to John Morearty and Eugene Rice for reading and thinking, to Robert Roy Wright for encouraging and editing, to Larry and Barbara Jackson and Sue Rice for understanding and laughing, to Wes and Hazel Brown for loving, to Douglas Moore for a lifetime, and to Weldon and Pat Crowley for dancing a little while.

Contents

Contents

Preface

Columbus, I am told, thought the world was round. He went sailing on the *Santa Maria* (good Christian, he) to prove it, opening up on that passage to India a new vastness, as they say—the riches of America.

He was wrong of course. The world sailed by saints is not round. It is square. It is a world they conquered but did not love. They came to Eden driven by the stark injunction to have dominion: with ramrods down their backs and iron in their crotches. St. Paul and John Calvin were their guides—men who copulated only to keep the race alive, who lived in Geneva and never once mentioned the Alps.

The myth of America has always been told as the story of freedom and adventure. Freedom for whom? The rhetoric of black power, of Chicano soul, of yellow panthers, of little big men in new tribal councils, might suggest that the revolutionary adventure of our time is the emergence of imprisoned minority groups into full shares of white middle-class opportunities. The proletariat (of whatever color) will rise, power adjudicated, social structures shifted, and mankind will be free.

But if all the social inequities were righted tomorrow, and fair systems devised for managing technocracy, we would not yet have rounded our world. Our square, disciplined, otherworldly psychic screen, our legacy from the chastity of Mary, the continence of Paul, the sterility of Calvin, still holds us prisoner.

There are many names for our prison: the establishment, the system, the man, the old culture, Consciousness I and II, inner-directedness, heteronomy. My own history names it "church," and the peculiar disability which it must perpetuate in order to function as authority for the whole history of Western man is called "transcendence."

Now the record of the "church" on social issues is shabby enough: too little and decorously tardy. Martin Luther King was fond of calling it the "taillight" of revolution. But even if synods, ecumenical councils, and annual conferences were seething with political radicals and raising the rabble with Tekoan "streams of righteousness," they would still be deeply implicated in the most regnant infelicity. They have anesthetized our bodies with an invidious combination of civilizing sexual restraint and rational social responsibility.

Not that we are celibate. Middle America still (*mutatis mutandis*) has sexual intercourse. It also has titillation as a tightly wound spring for orgasm, voyeurism as a substitute for reality, and mutual masturbation as surrogate intimacy. It is immobilized, rather than emancipated by its own fantasy life, because it cannot allow that imaginal sensuality to function as a proper lure for the human animal into sensuousness.

The human animal was, as all noble savages know, born to be free, but is everywhere in chains—and never so much as in Christendom. It is a particularly virulent incarceration here because, although it is self-inflicted, it is preached with the authority of creation itself, and guarded by that final cultural inflexibility that forces the animal into other worlds, that makes him an alien in his own land. Its final tragedy is that this is not a consciously demonic deflection, but simply ignorance of its own genius. It is not a failure of nerve, but a misreading of its heritage. "Christians" have not lacked courage (the Colosseum), industry (the Protestant ethic), or philosophical sophistication (the *Summa Theologica*). The tragedy of "culture Christianity" is that, concerning the core of its affirmation, it has been conspicuously "dumb."

Dr. Seuss was not on the lists with Dr. Reuben, "J," "M," and certainly not Wilhelm Reich, but his observations on the "flustards" could be a whimsical invocation to richer humanness—to sensuous Christianity:

> Of all the animals I've ever met
> The Flustards, I think, are the silliest yet.
> Poor Flustards! They spend every hour every day
> In front of their house in a most stupid way . . .
> Standing. Just standing. They're waiting, they say.
>
> But waiting for *what* . . . ?
> Well, they stare at the sky
> Looking for things that will NEVER come by . . .
> Like very small elephants
> Two inches high.
> They wait to see things that can't possibly come . . .
> Like five hundred bluebirds
> Inside a bass drum.
>
> They stand and wait for things like these:
> Steering wheels on apple trees
> And roller skates made out of cheese
> And peanuts floating in the breeze
> And three-cent stamps on bumble bees
> And thimbles on the thumbs of fleas
> And icicles that never freeze.
>
> They never have fun.
> Never play. Never run.
> They've never found out that it's terribly dumb
> Just to stand around waiting for things that can't come.*

This book is the celebration of one flustard who decided, at least, to stop staring.

---

* "The Flustards" by Dr. Seuss apeared in the August 1953 issue of *Redbook* Magazine. Copyright © 1953 by Theodor Geisel. Reprinted by permission of International Famous Agency.

Introduction: I Am Curious, Red, White, and Blue

My beloved land,
here I sit in London
    overlooking Regent's Park
    overlooking my new Citroën } both green
exiled by success of sorts.
I listen to Mozart
    in my English suit and weep,
        remembering a Swedish film.

JOHN UPDIKE, "Minority Report"
From *Midpoint and Other Poems* by John Updike. Copyright © 1963, 1969 by John Updike. Reprinted by permission of Alfred A. Knopf, Inc.

Now it is for the young men to encounter in such actions, and for me to give way to the persuasion of gloomy old age. But once I shone among the young heroes.

HOMER
The Iliad

In middle age . . . he believes he could avoid all the mistakes made decades before. It is his second chance, and he takes it—or tries to.

EDMUND BERGLER
The Revolt of the Middle-aged Man

13

In the summer of 1966 two remote and seemingly discontinuous events took place. First, my family and I came to California looking for "Fat City," and settled in what *Newsweek* called "the squalid backwaters of the San Joaquin" (Stockton), what *Sports Illustrated* called "Oxford on the Calaveras" (University of the Pacific). And second, a motion picture was shot in Sweden, screened under the intriguing title: *I Am Curious, Yellow.*

I Am Curious, Yellow (which I saw in London) was a frank, complex, and suggestive manifesto of change in Western styles of life. Young Lena Nyman, brutally honest and passionately probing the texture of her society and her own identity within that society, is the desperate, naked heroine of this unfolding of the Swedish flag, whose colors are yellow and blue. Lena *is* curious, so remarkably curious that her room is virtually a revolutionary archive, a collage of identities: piles of books, wall posters, newspaper clippings, even a portrait of Franco hanging in a gilded frame surrounded by a wilted laurel wreath. She keep boxes of files in alphabetical order to record her search: *R* for religion, for example (not much in it, she declares, but she's just getting started), *M* for men, and here apparently she was well on her way—with at least twenty-four lovers. Over her bed hangs her plaintive credo: I AM FREE.

We watch Lena uncover everything, including herself: problems of Swedish socialism, the emergence of the working class into the elusive classless society, the advocacy and ambivalence of nonviolence as a strategy for social change, including an actual interview with Martin Luther King when he was in Sweden raising money for his peace campaigns, the elucidation of various sexual styles (Western, Eastern, genital, oral, and something brand new: upside down in a tree—a position which can only be described as heroic!).

The film contains two very powerful clues as to where Western culture might be heading:

One was presented as the new ten commandments of a Swedish social guru named Lars Gyllensten. Since this is really a new age, contended Gyllensten, isn't it true that *God*'s commandments are out of date, that they have no more authority for young people?

Five of these commandments are actually given in the picture, two of which need to be stated plainly now.

1. "Thou shalt not have any other gods than provisionary ones," later translated, "Thou shalt worship only temporary gods." That is, nothing is final; all is momentary, fragmentary, and relative.

2. Gyllensten's searching sixth commandment: "Thou shalt not spread venereal diseases, or bring unwanted children into the world, or expose other people to sexual violence. Also, you should play your part in keeping the birth rate as low as possible, because altogether too many children are born. For the rest, you may devote yourself freely to sexual intercourse, masturbation, pornography, and such other good things of this kind as your animal nature, in its grace, may cause you to desire." The commandment is, as they say, crystal clear.

As a kind of mischievous seal on this physical and metaphysical challenge to tradition and the authority of the state, Lena and her twenty-fourth lover have intercourse on a bridge railing in front of the royal palace in Stockholm (young people in Sweden apparently have remarkable balance!), much to the comic chagrin of a palace guard, a young servant of the state who, in stealing glances at the view from the bridge, is obviously caught as most of us are between vicarious rebellion and institutional obedience.

The second powerful clue is a cinematic trick. Just as Lena and her lover (Borje) are conversing at the end of the movie and have succeeded in drawing us into their story, the director, the *actual* director, steps into the scene and unsettles us with his alien presence. It is never clear whether this is a movie within a movie or whether this trick brings us full cycle to the first of the picture where the director had appeared many times as part of the film about making a film. In fact, I distinctly got the feeling that *I* might have been filmed actually watching the movie of Swedish movie-making techniques. The point of this trickery is obscure, except that it is increasingly difficult in this exploding age to tell truth from appearance, fantasy from fact. When all authorities disintegrate and only temporary gods reign, we all become curious, yellow and blue, red, white, and blue.

But I have neglected that first remote event (our coming to

California), which lacks, shall we say, the range of interest and publicity of the second, but is not without some contribution to the texture of change. What I am about to share with you is deeply and unashamedly personal and just a trifle narcissistic. Any "straight" who would masquerade in print as an interpreter of our cultural revolution in Middle America is bound to be on the edge of something either therapeutic or neurotic. It may be in fact difficult for you to tell just when the author steps into the analysis and out again. It may even be difficult to separate imperative from rhetoric, for celebrations that *seem* one are always two. As the Swedish voices cry out at the beginning of the picture: "Buy our film, buy it. The only film that's shown in two editions. One yellow and one blue! Buy the yellow! Buy the blue! Buy our film because it's two. Exactly the same picture, yet so different."

My name is Lawrence. It is a solid name, with just the right suggestion of patrician ancestry; common, yet not too common. It has been used before with some honor and intrigue. A gentle man, whose worldly eye fixed the Coney Island of his mind by the lights of the city, uses it well. It pointed to the mystique of revolution in the sands of Arabia, and the exquisite coition with the godhead of energy for sons and lovers. The history of all of Europe was once in the hands of an Italian called the Magnificent. A little brother of the spirit declared himself in the presence of God sweeping houses, carrying water, and speaking softly to the ordinary ones—all in the name I bear.

I was called Lawrence by my father, for his brother, who never married and would not pass on his name. My eldest son struggles to find himself in the simple labyrinth of that name.

Lawrence, I have always felt, looked rather well with Meredith. Eight letters each with no middle problem name to mar that decently subtle symmetry. There are men and women whose full appellation can only be said to jar the sensibilities in scandalous fashion. A president of the University of Texas was named Theophilus Schickel Painter, and even using his first two initials couldn't hide that cacophonous disaster. I knew a girl once in grade school who was called Prunella Rottencrotch. Rumor has it that late in life she became a Dean of Women.

But Lawrence. Substantial, with mystery, and not without history. The ancient Greeks gave it birth, enshrining by its appropriate elegance the Olympic victor. It means "crowned with a wreath of laurels," the one who has run the race with discipline, whose body shines with endurance and strength, whose mind is incarnated skill, and who has won.

One recent September, returning from Callison College's India campus in Bangalore, I visited Athens and found myself in the modern Olympic stadium built to commemorate those ancient champions, and as the first site of the twentieth-century renewal of international competition. It was a typically clear, brightly lit Athenian day as my companion, Dr. Douglas Moore, provost of Callison, and I walked around the great track, listening to the silence of the centuries, and coming to rest before the winner's platform area. There on that spot was an obelisk statue of a male Greek—emblematic of the victor. He was crowned with a wreath of laurel and his body was all bare lines and graphic genitals.

There in that naked air, the long adult silence, the whitened magnitude of the past, I was seized with a primal desire to be me, to run as my brothers had run. So that September morning I stripped off my clothes and ran the Olympic track in Athens, and stood as proudly in the winner's circle as any ancient ever did.

Dr. Moore, having a certain decorous presence which prefers being arrested by an idea rather than by the police, did not join me. Instead he interrupted my moment of triumph by pointing out a busload of American tourists unloading for a look at the stadium. I should have run the track again, waving at the little old ladies as I went joggling by. That might have really widened the generation gap.

But no matter. For a moment—under the spell of Apollo, speeded by Hermes, and spirited by Dionysus, near the scent of the green bay tree—I was Lawrence.

I have been a minister with full credentials in the Methodist Church for twenty years, a college chaplain and a professor of religion for ten, a rectilinear being for forty. I learned very early to color within the lines, to do all things decently and in order, not to trust my own reactions, and to focus my perceptions by the lenses provided for me by our institutional initiations (family, church, school). Those lenses I found were hurting my eyes.

It is now apparent that Christianity as I had known it in Middle America and as it has been bodied forth in community standards, microformed in colleges like Pacific, is finished. Or rather, I would like to help finish it. The superstructure of worship has been fatally weakened and any external authority the church ever had is now painfully tenuous. We will continue to gather in church and college, of course, but the priests of both cultures have been defrocked. We are re-creating the garden scene: we have eaten of the tree of knowledge and see that we are naked. We have fallen upwards toward pure human decision where no imprimaturs are coercive. The ephemeral counter-culture—that intrusion of "centaurs" at the feast of technocracy—has exposed a society staggered by the inhuman weight of preformed authority: authority that sank into the quagmire of Vietnam, that shackled the blacks and the browns and the women of this land of the free, that turned our rivers into sewers and our clear day into heavy breathing night, that made us ashamed of our bodies, and so alienated us from physical affection that we loved only as competitors.

We are in an age of radical humanness, despite the talk of the "recovery of transcendence,"—an age void of any inherent values and meaning. This earth, with spectacular starkness, looks like a spaceship hurtling through limited time in unutterable magnitude. In our moments of lucidity we know ourselves to be alone and that all the exhilaration of moon walks and star treks only serve to heighten that sense of solitude: fifty billion dollars for forty pounds of dust and rocks, a technical presence in the world, and a trivialization of the mystery of creation with gargantuan golf shots. No, it was more than this. We know this earth now to be a green oasis in a vast sea of blackness.

What was begun so meekly by Galileo and Renaissance science has burst forth in man in profound, reluctant autonomy. Franz Kafka was right. Joseph K is on trial—but by whom? For what? There is nobody in charge, no judge in the castle, no heaven of ideas, no transcendent guarantee we call "God." There is man and the multiverse.

And there is me.

My name is Lawrence and I am married and I discovered and became ashamed of my body very early in life. Now my children discover theirs and wonder what earth is all about. How fragile their chances in our dominant goal-oriented American ethos, because earth isn't *about* anything at all—it *is*.

But this is not an elegy for a lost America, easily riding into a copout jeremiad. Misereres are part of celebrations too, but I want to play on other rhythms, and if hallelujahs are premature at least seize this time of my own history to reflect on the twin foci of a growing self: freedom and love.

Part I will deal with the pilgrimage of becoming free: resisting authority, emptying the past, deciding for today.

Part II will focus on loving release as consuming the provided value structure, the rebirth of receiving the world, and playing into the presence of every human moment.

I am not cynical. I am curious: about the center of gravity in the collegiate revolution, the nature of hippie withdrawal, the influence of Camus on the new sensibility, the new Harvey Cox, the old Hugh Hefner, the inner meaning of the Death of God controversy, the remarkable reception of *The Greening of America,* the apocalypse of Norman O. Brown, the transmutation of American heroes, the Jesus freaks, the emergence of the young as a new "stage" in life, the orgasm as worship, and theology as ecology. I am most curious about the possibility of setting the record straight on what constitutes a *Christian* self—on the sensory logic of the *Word* made *flesh.*

Young Lena was the heroine of two stories. One was yellow and the other blue. One was interesting and the other true. There is no guarantee that all of us will not simply project our wishes onto the real world, hoping somehow wildly to create the truth.

This is to be a double story. It is double twice: it is told in matching triads which suggest the developing self, and it defines this movement by both the inner and outer history of the radical revolution of the sixties.

Of course. Our sacred testaments are always two. It wasn't in sin that my mother conceived me, but in the very riddle of opposites: two embryonic symmetrical halves joined along the spine, stitched hastily at the last moment in the front, my very machinery for thinking split into two separate hemispheres. The struggle for salvation is literally the struggle for wholeness. We are all curious, divided beings.

I had to go all the way to Athens to fantasize my oneness—to run naked in the clear air and in the long silence, to be.

PART I

Freedom: The Apocalypse
of Intentionality

Zorba shook his head.

"No, you're not free," he said. "The string you're tied to is perhaps no longer than other people's. That's all. You're on a long piece of string, boss; you come and go, and think you're free, but you never cut the string in two. And when people don't cut that string . . ."

"I'll cut it some day!" I said defiantly, because Zorba's words had touched an open wound in me and hurt.

"It's difficult, boss, very difficult. You need a touch of folly to do that; folly, d'you see? You have to risk everything!"

NIKOS KAZANTZAKIS
Zorba the Greek

1

Resisting: From Bohemia to Utopia

There is, thank God, a limit to the meaningfulness of such a stereotyped characterization. It hits home in those areas where the college graduate has literally been stereotyped by his upbringing and by the rigid matrix of his schools. But it leaves out what makes him one individual, what makes him real. Doesn't he have a self beyond the stereotype? Isn't he, to use Timothy Leary's phrase, a two-billion-year-old carrier of the Light? Of course. But who sees it? His self has been scared into hiding. The stereotype that has been made of him hides his uniqueness, his inner life, his majesty from our eyes and, to a great extent from his own as well. He's got a sure A in Citizenship but he's failing in self-realization (a subject not too likely to appear in the curriculum).

JERRY FARBER
The Student as Nigger

A curious event of the late sixties was the popularity of the film, *The Graduate,* the viewing of which became almost a ritual for a wide spectrum of middle-class youth, who went to see it over and over. . . . *The Graduate,* like its paler predecessors, is a ritual of purification and cleansing, a celebration of the *capacity* of feeling to triumph over pattern. The interruption of a wedding ceremony—always a popular theme in American films—is not merely a suspense gimmick. It is what the film is all about: the battle between social forms and human feeling. And it is important that human feelings should occasionally win—

as important as occasional epiphanies and miracles are for religion. In
our society this issue is a matter of life and death . . .

PHILIP SLATER
The Pursuit of Loneliness:
American Culture at the Breaking Point

When I was a child I spoke like a child, I thought like a child, I
reasoned like a child, but when I became a man I gave up childish
ways.

PAUL OF TARSUS
Letter to the Corinthians

The Tribe of Benjamin

It takes no Delphic oracle to see the central issue of twentieth-
century man. It is freedom: freedom intellectually to pursue the
truth wherever it might lead and whatever traditions it might
shatter; freedom socially to be not merely persons to be counted
but persons who count and who may receive recognition com-
mensurate with skill and industry; freedom politically where all
men exercise in awareness of alternative possibilities for their
chosen state and where the will of the majority deliberately protects
the minority opposition.

It takes no royal seer to discern that these three freedoms rest
upon a fourth, a prior freedom, an *urfreedom,* a freedom so basic
that its articulation is actually a definition of freedom itself. It is
spiritual freedom: the fundamental emancipation of man which
allows him fullest development of his human possibilities. This is
not the absence of restraint, but the release of ability.

This is transcending freedom, quite distinguishable from coercive impress derived from "transcendence," which climbs across
the idols of the ecclesiastical tribe and stands in critical judgment
of every earthly authority. This is religious freedom, which enables
our ultimate commitment not to be identical with any institution,
any state, any catechism, any peer. It is prophetic freedom, which
challenges the prevailing drift of civilization in the name of God
and more centrally demands challenge to God himself: a freedom
whose civilizing standard is the norm by which the "good life" is

to be measured, and whose presence alone insures us against both "false freedom" (freedom to do what pleases us) and "false slavery" (freedom to do what pleases the state). It was harboring such thoughts as these that I went to the movies on a fine spring night in Stockton to see *The Graduate.*

Benjamin Braddock, having just been graduated with multiple honors from a prominent Eastern college, flies home to Los Angeles, seemingly ready for all the accolades our success society can bestow. But Benjamin withdraws—from the party in his home, from future plans, from social amenities. Into this void walks the wife of his father's best friend. She seduces him out of the depths of her own boredom and traps him into a new kind of curriculum. As the affair with Mrs. Robinson wears on, Benjamin finds new and genuine life with, of all people, her only daughter. Elaine is an undergraduate at Berkeley, and in that tense setting is faced with the realization of her mother's responsibility for the affair with Benjamin.

In icy, frenzied jealousy the Robinsons block Benjamin's future with Elaine by promoting her marriage to a young medical student—the epitome of stable, disciplined, and dedicated American youth.

In his own frenzy of decision and detective work, Benjamin discovers the date and place of Elaine's marriage and rushes to Santa Barbara—straight into the balcony of the First Presbyterian Church (*sic!* The ghost of Calvin walks) where the wedding processional has now ushered the entire party to the altar. He spreads his arms in wild agitation, like a giant moth, like an agony of crucifixion, then slams the balcony glass and cries: "Elaine! Elaine! Elaine!"

Benjamin's shout rips apart the liturgy of convenience. His ringing "No!" throws down the gauntlet of confrontation. Rushing to the altar, he seizes Elaine, strikes Mr. Robinson, picks up the cross from the altar and swings it wildly, terrorizing the bridegroom and immobilizing the clergy. Then in an excruciating benediction he locks the church with the cross. The new, bizarre, exorcized couple board a city bus headed for Morgan Street and insist that the stunned driver get it moving.

Now the meeting of man and moment allowed this understanding to be present: you are free and you are responsible (capable of responding), and what awakens your freedom is your joy in finding another self you richly like, and what activates your "responsibility" is the desire to share with that other whatever you actually are. Or, rather, simply to be with that other.

Let us concede that as commercial enterprise *The Graduate* was slick, professional, too much Andy Hardy *redivivus,* and certainly not intentionally theological. The fact remains that it was received as a parable of liberation, a prismatic event where freedom was refracted. The colors that followed became darkly elegiac (*Easy Rider*), mutedly wistful (*Alice's Restaurant*), classically atomized (*Five Easy Pieces*). But *The Graduate* was invested as myth.

He came with all the paraphernalia of emancipation: a lauded diploma, acceptances into the prestigious professional schools, jet-carried into the city of the angels, an athletic conqueror of distances and discipline, an honored son in the tribe of emerging manhood. Yet he was as much in bondage as all the ancient tribes of Israel down in Egypt land. He was utterly enclosed: surrounded by faces in the jet, suffocated by parties, stuffed ludicrously into a frogman suit (on his twenty-first birthday!), flapping helplessly in a swimming pool—much like the aimless aggressions of the angel fish in his father's home aquarium (with his vision even more narrowly proscribed in a sloshing face mask). And as the final devastation of his failure to choose to be, he was ushered into the sanctuary of sex not by his own peers, but by the jaded temptress whose appetite for ecstasy is titillated by a boy, and satisfied by no one.

I was not misled by the name. Mrs. Robinson was my dean at Southwestern University. Mrs. Robinson was my fifth-grade teacher at Calvert, Texas. Mrs. Robinson was my bishop in New England. Mrs. Robinson was my mother. She is the womb of the world disguised as friend. She is the trustee who gives us birth and smothers us in swaddling clothes. She is the college that issues forth the graduate without confronting him with his own humanity.

No wonder she grew edgy when Benjamin wanted widened intercourse, wanted to talk about who she was, how she had been forced into marriage by conceiving on the back seat of a car. That

human absurdity would shatter her citadel of ennui, would allow
Benjamin to see her truly naked and move him toward deep passion—where human persons involve themselves in each other's
lives.

I am not fooled by the name Mrs. Robinson. She is Satan, the
final temptation to be passive, to be tool, to be thing. And I am
not self-righteous about this. Mrs. Robinson is also me: middle-
aged, dragging forty years over the earth, fading, grasping for
youth, using youth to feed the hunger never filled by awe before
the multiverse—widening the gap between those who would experience life and those who would symbolize the experience.[1] *

But the fair Elaine comes, issued forth by the very power that
would continue to enslave the graduate, as dragon teeth sown
spring up on occasion to slay the monster parent. Elaine becomes
redeemer not because she dies bravely, but because she feels
deeply. She knows humiliation when being used in a cheap strip
joint, knows simple warm communion over a sandwich, knows outrage triggered by innocence offended.

Elaine is nothing other than the fair Elaine. The Elaine in the
Lancelot myth was unable to cope with Merlin's magic, but this
Elaine is redeemer because she provides the occasion for Benjamin's first true decision to become a man. And the setting for
this decision? The graduate decides in *Berkeley* to take this
gracious gift of woman. Within the very arena of university revolt
where the undergraduates ground the wheels of man's convention
to a halt and opened a new era in education, admonished a world
to tell it like it is, there in the upper room of a tiny hotel Benjamin
confronts Elaine and her father with the truth about Mrs. Robinson. And it is also the truth about himself.

In the climactic scene that unfolds in the church, the symbols
of authority are everywhere: the smartly dressed mother, the
father of the bride, the doctor, the black-robed cleric, the ancient
liturgies, all tightly woven together by the rolling sounds of the
organ.

Then there is the shout of salvation. Elaine! A man strikes the

* Superior figures refer to Notes at end of text.

father, takes up the cross, locks the church. The bus rolls off into uncertainty.

"God bless you, Mrs. Robinson," sang Simon and Garfunkel. It was an opening, a door, like a bridge over troubled waters.

We have been subtly taught to be silent when faced with an actual affirmation of freedom, a lived liberation, a resurrecting spontaneity that cannot be contained, categorized, that will not be predicted. We are systematically schooled to believe that life begins sometime in the future, like Sartre's professor in *The Age of Reason* who was always waiting for something he could get his teeth into and found at last that he had never bitten into anything at all. Toothless and passionless, our life ends—and long before we do. Why do we allow it to be so?

The source of our self-inflicted imprisonment is our symbolization of that future-goal-oriented mentality. Tomorrow *I* will be the authority that I rebel against today. But there is always *another* authority beyond that we have just overcome, like an infinite regress of status symbols that can never be reached. I never get out of the system of authority; becoming what I deplore only insures my ultimate enslavement.

So we settle for plastic, Disneyland adventure, an insulated flirtation with reality, for to exercise freedom means that life must always be lived in the present with such awareness that the only paralysis of action would be a paralysis of possibilities. Thus we continue to deny our heritage, Christian *and* American, for a pot of message. And the message is everywhere: look to the past, remember how it was, lower our anxieties by allegiance to the liturgies of yesterday, keep in step with the endless line of patriotic splendor. What we *will* be is always drawn out of the assumptions of what we *were*.

One recalls the hillbilly in Tennessee who refused to move out of the house his father had built, in spite of the impending flood by the TVA. He said that he had promised not to let "his father's fire go out." We all have a nourished nostalgia for that faithful son. We have a natural attraction for the past, we who are born, bred, and buttered in America, who love mother and apple pie, who hate communists, who get exponential goose bumps when we hear the purple majesties of "America the Beautiful," who feel a shiver of hope in inauguration banalities of togetherness. Certainly we do live out of a concrete memory, but our real past is not a reproducible tableau. What irony that we should define our heritage in terms of what once was!

The grave at the Old North Bridge in Concord should have made that clear. There where two British soldiers are buried, James Russell Lowell's words are written on stone:

> Across three thousand miles they came
> To keep the past upon the throne.

There is no greater tragedy than when we die at the foot of the bridge that crosses over into the present. The American revolution of the sixties brought new graves and the tragic realization that between the now and the then there could be no compromise at all.

The Revolting Campus

The Benjamin myth has already used Berkeley as part of its general frame, and probably incidentally. But the crisis of authority erupted there in the fall of 1964, and, despite the momentary cynical—or contemplative—calm, will not be resolved until the solid middle in this country experience that same crisis. The collegiate explosion was made inevitable by the interface between accelerating technical research and the bizarre, relentless "logic" of the humanities. These two elements set off against each other like the two sides of the San Andreas fault, and sometime, somewhere on that line, the cultural seismograph would register wildly. The crack (we called it unhappily and inaccurately and quite perversely a generation gap) widened, and will continue to widen again. And if all is quiet now, and houses of excellence built again, they will not last. Day after tomorrow slippage will occur along that interface and governors will call out the troops. To put the matter with formal bluntness: the fault is fascism, our acquiescence to centralized authority which postpones selfhood in the name of order.

Revolt on the college campus, of course, wasn't new. In 1766 Harvard students rebelled after being served bad butter, and students at the University of Paris in the twelfth century moved from the Continent to Oxford, England, to establish a newer, freer university. In A.D. 385, tired of being badgered by student dissidence, a young teacher left Carthage for Rome, where the students were better behaved—even if worse at paying their fees. Living through campus unrest probably helped Augustine become a saint. Exactly two generations ago a small Midwestern college was forced to a standstill by a student boycott of classes, a boycott so successful that it forced the president to resign. That student revolt was led by a young athlete named Ronald Reagan.

But the turmoil in the sixties had at its center an issue so far-reaching that if the revolution ever coalesces and succeeds, our society will be radically altered, not only in its structure, but more fundamentally in its consciousness. What Charles Reich calls romantically "the greening of America" started as a civil rights protest, escalated into a Free Speech Movement, and continued as a Free America Movement. Those who began the movement probably had no idea that their protest was a total confrontation with our civilized failure to be free.

As a kind of ironic salute to American bureaucracy, letter groups spawned by the movement sprang up everywhere: SNCC (Student Nonviolent Coordinating Committee), which eventually produced nonviolent leaders such as H. Rap Brown and Stokely Carmichael, SDS (Students for Democratic Society), FSM (Free Speech Movement), and SPASM (Society for the Prevention of Asinine Student Movements). Methodism's Garrett Seminary in Evanston, Illinois, became excited enough to form a group called CHANGE (Christian Heretics Agitating for New Garrett Education). They, of all people, should have remembered that Luther never intended to destroy the Roman Church.

Word even got out to tiny, typically mid-American, Albion College in Michigan. An excellent school academically, it was still locked into another era socially: no drinking on campus, sign in and sign out for women, and the rest of it. There was, I recall, a beautiful black woman who walked out of the jungles of Angola to get to Albion, and there had to sign out to go across the street!

In the spring of 1964, Joseph Mathews, dean of the Ecumenical Institute of Chicago, appeared there as the featured speaker in what was called the "Ventures in Meaning" series, quickly initialed VIM—students just as quickly found a detergent *and* a magazine for homosexuals named VIM. Several years later the president changed the name to "Religion in Imaginative Perspective" (RIP), and, after authority-ridden students had their fun with this, the collegiate version of the old-fashioned revival week was dropped altogether.

Dean Mathews is still one of the most widely used speakers on college campuses, and has a platform style utterly unique and shamelessly pirated by his own staff at the Institute. Years ago he developed a technique for capturing student attention. Invited to Amherst in the days of David King's chaplaincy, he asked how long he had to speak. King replied: "About ten seconds." Mathews, understanding as all men of charisma understand, started his speech from his chair and continued speaking as he walked, not into the pulpit, but into the audience. He hasn't been in a pulpit since.

Now Albion had a required chapel-convocation sequence: fourteen hundred students jammed into the chapel sometimes *twice* a week and most of them conspicuously against their will. The requirement quite naturally had become a symbol of administration authoritarianism. So, after he was introduced, Dean Mathews walked out to the edge of the front row, looked up at the fractious throng present under much coercion, and hoarsely intoned: "If there's anything that makes me angry, it's a college administration that treats its students like children."

The students exploded. When they were quiet, Mathews added, even more hoarsely: "But if there's anything that makes me angrier, it is students who allow themselves to be treated like children!"

Albion College was never the same again.

None of the colleges are the same. That "silent generation" of the fifties accelerated from vocal to volcanic and the campus (which once meant "playground") became in many places virtually an armed camp with battle lines drawn between students' militant

nonnegotiable demands, administrative orderly intransigence, and
the atmosphere filled with obscene ritual chants: "On strike. . . .
Shut it down. . . ." The explosive youth culture was a major campaign issue in the 1968 Presidential election, symptomatic of the
stark fact that the campus crisis jangled the nerves of a whole
nation, nerves finally shattered by the massive student protests
over the Cambodian "intrusion," the killings at Kent State and
Jackson State. The Mayday weekend in the spring of 1970 at Yale
brought full circle the confrontation consciousness of the sixties, as
all factions of the movement (Black Panthers, Students for Democratic Society, Young Americans for Freedom, police, clergy,
college faculty *and* administration) came together to *prevent* mass
destruction. It was a signal that the revolution—which had moved
from West to East in an ironic reversal of the American Dream—
had stalemated.

The literature on the student mind grew to overwhelming pro-
portions, ranging from frighteningly frank underground provoca-
tion such as *The Student as Nigger,* journalese treatments like
Time magazine, substantial scholarly debates (*Atlantic Monthly*
series, particularly Fall and Winter, 1968–69), to vast psychological analyses (Kenneth Keniston's *The Uncommitted Young Radicals,* or *No Time for Students: Growth and Restraint in College
Students* and *A Study of the Varieties of Psychological Development,* edited by Joseph Katz of Stanford University's Institute for
the Study of Human Problems [2]). Even *Together* magazine once
took time out from watching the sun go down to print a piece
called "Unrest on the Campus" by Carol Doig. One of the more
inspired *Esquire* issues was dedicated to the "Super-students" who
control the campus, and featured super-college-heroes such as
Joan Baez (who later married super-student officer and slinger of
stones at "Goliath," David Harris), Marvel Comics, and the
denizens of Middle-Earth. This kind of madness reached its nadir
when Ayn Rand stopped embracing John Galt long enough to
write a blistering critique of the whole campus mood entitled,
"The Cashing In: The Student Rebellion" (*The New Left: Anti-
Industrial Revolution*) in which she identifies the grand culprit
behind the contemporary chaos as—are you ready?—Immanuel
Kant.

What was this all about?

The full answer would be extremely complex. But it is non-debatable that a *central* word—with pregnant incantation—was *freedom*. As Dr. Edmund Williamson, dean of students at the University of Minnesota, summarized, "The most important freedom of all is to be taken seriously, to be listened to."

Students in the sixties literally became part of the American social revolution. They lined up with a remarkable series of freedom movements, the Boston Tea Party, the abolitionists' campaign, women's suffrage, the labor revolution, the veterans' rebellion, and the black revolution. To this list the students of the early seventies have added the most radical revolution of them all, women's liberation. "Most observers agree," wrote Paul Denise, "that it began with the Southern sit-in movement in 1960." Freedom riding, House Un-American Activities Committee demonstrations, peace marching, the enthusiastic student response to the Peace Corps, research of student political movements both left and right, the energetic launching of a new wave of student projects ranging from Crossroads Africa to Acción in Latin America—these were all cited as evidence of an almost universally heralded new student activism.

> O Freedom, O Freedom, O Freedom over me. . . .
> Before I'd be a slave
> I'd be sleeping in my grave,
> And go home to my Lord and be free.

If the black man could move for freedom, why not the student? Jerry Farber was later to remind both how much they had in common.

This drive for self-regulation was the core of the black studies and Third World curriculum demands (e.g., San Francisco State and Cal-Berkeley). It was part of the new racial identity strategy that translated into the general word "power." The militant students simply no longer tolerated *not* being listened to. "Scooter" Aiken, a black leader of the strikers at San Francisco State, a 3.7 prelaw senior and sometime ghetto rhetorician, reported (in sinuously provocative street language) that reasonable requests for a separate ethnic studies department had been shunted aside for over two-and-a-half years before the strike became the only available method for focusing attention on the irrelevant nature of California State College education to minority problems. John Lindsay (his Republican mooring already endangered by heavy urban seas) addressed the National Association of College Academic Deans in Pittsburgh, January 1969, and defended the Columbia rebellion as the climax of six years of frustrated attempts by serious students to get adequate reform of the curriculum, a position brilliantly documented in another confessional, *The Strawberry Statement, Notes of a College Revolutionary,* by Columbia's wry radical, James Simon Kunen. This is one of the reasons why the students added to the litany of freedom the sacred imperative, *Now.* When students sensed the administration playing games with their seriousness they introduced a coarseness to their hymnic chants: Bulllllllllshit! As they added tantrums of immediacy they were labeled at best irrational ("I just can't understand these kids") and at worst actual gangsters (as S. I. Hayakawa still calls them: "racketeers").

The most *minimal*—one might say trivial—motivation behind the revolution of the sixties was simply that the student was trying desperately to grow up, to throw off the insulation of parents: to transcend adolescence. And everywhere in college he saw himself hemmed in, required to death, honed and dormed and housemothered to distraction. How long can a man endure in a frogman's suit? Even when academic freedom was allowed there was this maddening preoccupation with rules. Until the last of the sixties at Oxford the gates closed every night at 11 P.M., just as they had been closing since before the fourteenth century, and students still spent time issuing privately printed material to show fellow students just where the walls were vulnerable after nocturnal activities. At Yale since 1880 it had been the custom to wear a coat and tie to dinner and naturally no Yalie could break this tradition, although it was whispered snidely that some came in coat and tie over T-shirt and underwear. The *Saturday Review* reported that the most persistent reason for students transferring to downtown universities like NYU was the "stifling provincial character" of many small-time colleges. A Colby student said, "I was cramped, bored, and disappointed. I didn't care for the narrow existence. The big event of the week was when the *New York Times* would come up the hill." The irony was that the more open and excellent the education, the more likely the college was to produce dissident students, since if they were trained to think for themselves, they might actually start thinking—and being. Then when the dissidence level rose in the urban academic jungle, these levels of alienation drove many students back to the bucolic settings from which they had escaped!

Of course the issue was more than social and civil freedom. Academic freedom was also a primary concern. It will be increasingly in jeopardy in the seventies. A college is not a college unless the full spectrum of opinion is open to the students. "Opinion" ought not even to be modified by "responsible" if this latter word is taken in its ordinary usage as an establishment code word implying predigested goals in league with the system. Colleges by any radical critique were not to be rites of passage or initiatory forms: precise ablutions of the "maturing" mind. Apparently Middle America's image of education was much more standard cookie cut. This was the burden of Eric Solomon's protest concerning curricular regimentation:

> When I left Ohio State after six years in the wake of almost one third of my department who have for a variety of reasons taken other appointments, and after I had helped initiate a lawsuit against the president and the board of trustees, I [had finally] learned that good salaries, light teaching loads, and air conditioned offices are no substitutes for a full measure of academic freedom.[3]

When the president of Emory University stood behind Thomas Altizer in the controversy that burst over the "death of God" in Georgia, it was estimated that Emory in that embattled stand lost over ten million dollars in potential contributions. Said the president, "I wish such excitement were happening in all the departments of this college." (Referring, I take it, to the controversy, *not* the contributions.)

That kind of freedom on the college campus represents, of course, a real threat to safe, sequestered, doctrinaire education.

Almost all college administrations for propaganda purposes will claim freedom for their campuses. Prospective loss of funds tends to tarnish enthusiasm for freedom. As one president put it: "You can do anything you want to on this campus, as long as it's in good taste."

Students are flesh and not to be canonized, but for one ambient moment in our history they would not be dehumanized. That silent generation sat around listening to commencement speakers— and finally started taking *them* seriously. One such address is of more than passing interest, given the Columbia moment of truth, the Berkeley riots, and the reintroduction of the *service* concept into American higher education by practical administrations and entrepreneurial faculty.

ON STUDENT MILITANTS: Far from discouraging your students' social and public interests, I propose that you positively exploit them.

Here is an honorable source of college spirit; here is a worthy unifying and organizing principle for your whole campus life.

I say: thank God for the spectacle of students picketing—even when they are picketing me at Sacramento and I think they are wrong—for students protesting and freedom-riding, for students listening to society's dissidents, for students going out into the fields with our migratory workers, and marching off to jail with our segregated Negroes.

At last we're getting somewhere. The colleges have become boot camps for citizenship—and citizen leaders are marching out of them.

For a while, it will be hard on us administrators. Some students are going to be wrong, and some people will want to deny them the right to make mistakes. Administrators will have to wade through angry letters and colleges will lose some donations. We Governors will have to face indignant caravans and elected officials bent on dictating to state college faculties.

But let us stand up for our students and be proud of them.

If America is still on the way up, it will welcome this new, impatient, critical drop of young gadflies. It will be fearful only of the complacent and passive.

—From Governor Edmund G. Brown's
Commencement Address at the
University of Santa Clara, June, 1961.[4]

In 1964 the chickens came home to roost. In 1966 the chickens were roasted. In 1968 the chickens turned into hawks for the right to be doves.

Hair Like Lamb's Wool

In the fall of 1968 a paradigm incident of participatory relevant education signaled just how seriously some contemporary students took Governor Brown. Berkeley students designed, with faculty approval, a course to explore—along with other aspects of our society's disintegration and possible regeneration—the dimensions of the present racial crisis, a course called Social Analysis 139X. Since part of the analysis dealt with the black revolution, the students invited someone to lecture who might possibly *know* something intimate about this revolution. They invited Eldridge Cleaver.

Now while they could have listened to some sociologist who had ridden through Harlem on a subway, published thirty surveys of slum problems, and even had his picture taken with an actual black man (without a ripple from the California public I would guess), the students chose the leader and national symbol of black militancy. The establishment's response to this inspired piece of contemporaneity was to ban the course for credit if Cleaver lectured more than once (he was asked to give ten lectures), and to cause the regents to pass five resolutions aimed at Cleaver but in effect seriously undercutting the academic freedom of the university.

This incendiary action from both sides was typical of the sixties, for the meaning of freedom was not always understood with any richness by either the radicals or the reactionaries. There were certainly two competing ideas of freedom operating in these confrontations, ideas whose broad lines go back as far as Plato. John Hallowell, professor of political science at Duke University, underlines the seminal reference in the dialogue *Gorgias*. There Socrates and Callicles are debating the meaning of freedom. Callicles represents many a college student when he says that the good life is the gratification of desire and that freedom is simply the opportunity to get what you want, the ability to do as you please. Socrates counters with the argument that if man simply attempts to satisfy his desire he is doomed to a life of frustration, for men, in his analogy, are like leaking casks that never can be filled. The man who does what he pleases is not free, but a slave to his passions. He will think he chooses without hindrance, but his appetites will in fact consume him. So, says Socrates, freedom consists in disciplining ourselves to achieve the perfection of the human possibility.

There was—to look at the matter straight on—this strain of sheer recalcitrance, a maverick motif on the campus, a reversion to Halloweenish pranks, a letting off of steam, a nostalgia for turbulence (what Elmer Gantry would call "stretching room"), a goof-off period which *was* in Carl Oglesby's phrase: "a temper tantrum." Some adolescents of whatever age want to disestablish the establishment for the hell of it (reminds one of a recent book), turn over college presidents like you would turn over old garbage cans, join the revolution for personal therapy. Wallace Hamilton, late pastor of the famed Pasadena Community Church in Florida, wrote about these rebels without a cause.

> The most publicized are the rebels without a cause, the bored, the beaten, the defiant ones in whom the spirit of rebellion is wholly negative. It goes nowhere and does nothing but rebel for the sake of rebellion. I heard of a little four-year-old boy who every day would cross the street to his grandmother's house, step inside the door, and boldly shout, "Grandma, I won't." [5]

A great many adults across the country nodded in agreement with Hamilton, including a very large nod from the capital in Sacramento (a form of penance I suppose for early Midwestern audacity), and a standing ovation from Alabama. Dr. Max Rafferty nearly rode grandma's "No" into the U.S. Senate.

Some "rebels" would probably agree, too, if they would take out time from conforming to nonconformity to face themselves. Warren Martin, former Provost of Raymond College, now one of the directors of the Research Center for Higher Education at Berkeley, and author of two tomes—well, one tract and one tome!—on innovative education (one promising *Alternatives to Irrelevance,* and the other much more realistically—cynically?—

seeing nothing in the land but *Conformity*), wrote an earlier assessment of the new student ferment titled "Has the Revolution a Future?" He warned then that we should not be lured into the comforting belief that we have changed basically because we have grown a beard. For all its apparent impressiveness, a beard represents change more than it does growth, and, quoting Charles O'Conner of the University of Chicago, Martin continues:

> Don't mistake social gracelessness for genuine intellectual conformity. Do not confuse Bohemia with Utopia. Don't let cocktail conversation about Kierkegaard and Camus pass for scholarship. One of the realities of the educated life, unfortunately, is that scholarship, genuine scholarship, however exciting its results, involves a necessary preface of drudgery, long hours of patient "digging." [6]

Translate this into the drug scene as don't mistake hallucination for vision, and into the student rebellion as don't mistake hostility for critique. And, incidentally, translate this into the suburban scene as don't mistake insulation for responsibility.

But even such immaturity as Martin is describing (Martin himself later grew a beard and discarded his old pictures of John Wesley!) finds a defender of the eminence of Paul Tillich. In his second collection of sermons, *The New Being,* Tillich speaks of the necessity of students cutting the ties with family and asks the question, "Is it willfulness which demonically disrupts the family communion, or is it a step toward independence and one's own understanding?" [7] Tillich confesses that we never know the answer for certain, but also insists that we must take the risk of this emancipation, even though it necessarily takes in the beginning the form of rebellion. Then he concludes:

> But do not mistake me! Opposition and revolt are not yet freedom. They are unavoidable stages on the way to freedom, but they create another servitude if they are not overcome as much as the early dependence must be overcome.[8]

In fact, the time of sheer rebelliousness was, of all things, institutionalized in a college, baptized by a Catholic order, and a girl's school at that. It was Marymount Manhattan College, where nearly six hundred girls recited prayers before class, organized slum dwellers in the extracurriculum, and had rebellion praised by their mother superior, President M. Joyce Egan. The school's philosophy appears on a collage just inside the entrance: "Youth is a time of rebellion. Rather than squelch the rebellion one might better enlist the rebels to join the greatest rebel of all time—Christ himself." [9]

There is an ancient, apocryphal tale which dramatizes this necessity of rebellion. I say "apocryphal" although Jerome Hines, recounting his early experiences at the Met, claims that something very much like this really did happen. It seems that the Metropolitan Opera was doing *Faust* and on opening night the tenor, a very rotund singer, came to the last act ready to pay his debt to Mephistopheles by descending into Hell. "Hell" was to be entered through (how else?) a trap door on the stage, and as the wide-angled singer descended he got stuck halfway down. The spear carriers pushed and Mephistopheles pulled, but Faust was stuck. A hush fell over that sophisticated New York audience—an awkward silence, broken only when a little man jumped up in the top row of the balcony and shouted, "Hallelujah! Hell's full!"

I can believe it: balconies are such tempting platforms for shouting. But there is a profound sense in which we ought to be saying to students everywhere, "Hallelujah! Hell's full!" Risk mistakes, risk accidents, embrace the threat of moving from heteronomy to autonomy. Let the college become an arena of doubt, examine all the assumptions, all the "answers," insist that the campus become a laboratory for revolt, a new *ecclesia,* an overground underground. The old *ecclesia,* before it became frozen with piety and transcendent reassurances, *was* the center of revolution. Wendell Phillips, archaeologist, student of William F. Albright, and vastly courted potential benefactor (he is the world's richest oil concessionaire), is writing (with fourteen outstanding biblical scholars) a new interpretation of Jesus, attempting to establish that the Nazarene was put to death as a rebel against the Roman state as a Zealot. Whatever the book's merits as scholarship, it will make for great rhetoric: with hair like lamb's wool and feet like burnt brass (you dig?), black Jesus flayed the establishment and became a cult hero to a generation both rebellious and redemptive.

So freedom as license and freedom as discipline: this was a central ambivalence in the student revolt. Students who were "doing their thing" were not always careful to protect those who "dug" another thing. I marched with the strikers at San Francisco State and listened to the mass rally that blocked Sater Gate, and being from Texas, knew a brush arbor revival spirit when I felt it. Riots, if we are going to tell it like it is, are fun. The physical dangers, the arrests, the deprivations, the instant martyrdom, the intransigent polarizations, the realities of something tangible happening—even death—are exhilarating for both sides. Freedom can easily become a code word for welcome chaos, allowed breast-beating outraged clichés to substitute for genuine discussion of issues, and in fact block not merely gates but decision itself. This is why Sidney Hook, professor of philosophy at New York University and close analyst of the student revolution since Berkeley '64, founded an organization to deal with that academic crisis. He calls it the University Center for Rational Alternatives. Wrote Dr. Hook:

> We need—and I know this sounds paradoxical—to counterpose to the revolt of the emotionally committed the revolt of the rationally committed. . . . In the long run, the preservation of democracy depends upon a passion for freedom, for the logic and ethics of free discussion and inquiry, upon refusal to countenance the measures of violence that cut short the processes of intelligence upon which the possibility of shared values depends.[10]

As a dean of the chapel at two widely separated church-related colleges, I was charged with the responsibility for arranging a curricular program and chapel sequence that addressed the revolutionary demand for campus—for human—freedom. Under the aegis of this credo—my version of a center for "rational alternatives"—I lived out a vocation in the turbulent decade just past:

> We do not wish to indoctrinate, but to educate, that is, to probe our assumptions about ourselves as communal, culturally conditioned

human beings, and provide the opportunity for intelligent, open, and prepared exercise of our commitments.

This is the college of worship: in reverent self-understanding and response. The freedom necessary to risk such a program we take to be a profound legacy of the Christian faith.

I wrote this as liberal rhetoric. I felt, as every decent citizen did, that if we could just get the radicals and the conservatives together that a consensus would emerge and the newly energized community would move perceptively forward intact. After all, Hook and Aristotle had to be correct: man is rational as well as political. The radicals would see that freedom cannot be license, the conservatives would see that freedom cannot be sheer internalized discipline, and the states, as always, would be united.

A sumptuous meal—eating those words.

St. Timothy and the Gospel of LSD

"Free," I soon discovered, was an uncompromising adjective in the same way that "love" is an absolute noun. Peter Berg, one of the chief Diggers (he would quickly disclaim this), founder of the Free Store in the Haight-Ashbury district of San Francisco, used to explain the "ontology" of the hippie dream with that adjective. On campus to discuss rock music and youth alienation, he said point-blank, "Man is free." To understand the nature of the movement, he insisted, take any word at all, and put "free" in front of it. So "free" store, "free" college, "free" music, "free" love, "free" people.

This may sound almost childishly naïve, but one remembers that St. Francis indulged in precisely this redemptive simplicity. He said that, to understand the nature of his movement, we should take any word and put "brother" in front of it. So "brother" tree, "brother" sun, "brother" man. And one day near evening, "brother" death.

It should not have been surprising, then, that chapel became a matrix of revolution on campus, confronting the academic community with its own history, and, consistent with its Christian per-

spective which is *radical freedom,* insist that the college be what
it is: a playground of liberation.

It was this understanding of the nature of worship (i.e., what is
worth doing?) that brought me in contact with a most weird evan-
gel: Dr. Timothy Leary.

I met Leary in January of 1967, five months after he had announced the formation of his religious community in which the
communicants ingested their own communal initials. He called it
the *L*eague for *S*piritual *D*iscovery, and became its self-proclaimed
prelate. In 1968 he published the "Old Testament" of this league
under the title *High Priest,* as well as a spiritual handbook entitled
The Politics of Ecstasy. I had invited Leary to speak on his experience with drugs as a sacred communal rite.

The college and community went into an absolute frenzy when
they heard of the invitation. Leary in chapel! One would have
thought that I had asked the devil himself.[11] The threatening nature
of Leary's presence was revealed in this letter to the president from
Monterey:

> In general, controversial advocates in the field of political philoso-
> phy, or social, theological, and moral questions should be heard and
> not suppressed. The inquiring mind is not harmed by exposure to
> new ideas, even though unpopular or unorthodox. Communists,
> Birchers, American Nazis, and atheists can be heard and evaluated.
> [But not Timothy Leary, for he "is selling something which is thus far
> considered by responsible authorities to be physically, emotionally,
> and mentally dangerous to the individual, as well as illegal."]
>   If the *Pacific Weekly* is accurate, "As the audience arrives, psyche-
> delic music and perhaps lighting will set the mood. . . ." One might
> conjecture whether Larry Meredith will be seated cross-legged in a
> cloud of smoke intoning an invocation. [I wasn't. I was reading
> sonorously from I Timothy!]

Even *Ramparts* Magazine took notice, commenting in a major
article that Timothy Leary was off in some nowhere place like
Stockton, trying to turn on little old Methodist ladies in drip-dry
dresses. *Sic transit gloria mundi!* [12]

Now to a naïve and unreflective bourgeois man the relationship between drugs and religion may not only seem absurd, but posi- tively perverse. Yet a glance at the history of religion will show that man has always seen the connection between ingesting chemi- cals and performing bodily actions which alter states of conscious- ness, producing what has been known as the mystical religious experience: the *kykeon* eaten and drunk on the sixth day of the Eleusinian mysteries in ancient Greece, the pituri of the Australian aborigines, the tea of Zen Buddhism that calls to the realm of the immortals, the cult of the vision of Dionysus, the soma of the Hindus, Mexico's two-thousand-years-old "sacred mushrooms" which are translated into Aztec as "God's flesh," not to mention the wine used in the Eucharist and the Seder Feast of the Jews. The North American (Indian) church is officially recognized and sanctioned as using peyote for its communion.

In fact, Henri Bergson, French philosopher of "creative evolu- tion" suggested that ancient "dynamic religion" was induced chem- ically, and Mary Barnard, in the *Phi Beta Kappa Journal* in 1963, predicted that "Theo-botanists" in fifty years could make a great deal of "precious" doctrine out of date.

Leary, as a theo-psychologist, came on with impressive creden- tials (a doctorate from Berkeley, a research post at Harvard, a serious publishing record with suitably innocuous academic titles such as "The Effects of Test Feedback on Creation Performance and of Drugs on Creative Experience," and "Drugs, Set, and Sug- gestibility," as well as the Introduction to David Solomon's solid anthology on LSD). That his interest in the religious implication of drugs antedated his legal problems is amply supported by an article which he published in 1963 on the subject in *Religious Education* and an address with the same substance which he deliv- ered to a conference of Lutheran psychologists of the American Psychological Association. There was genuine religious fervor in what he said then:

Is your religious advisor talking from direct experience, or simply repeating clichés? . . . Do his words spring from a spiritual or from a secular point of view? Is he motivated by a dedicated quest for answers to basic questions, or is he protecting his own psychological position, his own secular game? . . . How would the debate sound to you if you were fatally diseased with a week to live, and thus less committed to secular issues? . . . *Is the point of view one which opens up or closes down?* (Italic added.) Are you being urged to explore, experience, gamble out of spiritual faith, join someone who shares your cosmic ignorance on a collaborative voyage of discovery? . . . If he is against what he calls "artificial methods of illumination," ask him what constitutes the natural. Words? Rituals? Tribal customs? Alkaloids? . . . If your advisor is against LSD, what is he for? [13]

Leary was for freedom, the freedom to experience the expansion process in human affairs. Expansion in physics and biology he understood in evolutionary terms. But social evolution was to be measured by increased freedom, both external and internal. In his manifesto for freedom written with his Harvard colleague, Baba Ram Dass (née Richard Alpert), he litanized this as

Freedom to step out of the tribal game and move to construct a new social form. Freedom to move in space. Freedom to experience. Freedom to explore.[14]

Leary then hinted at his own vocation for the future, a model well suited to fill the vacuum left by the demise of Superman, the spare realism of Promethean man, the disillusioned patriot, the guilt-ridden playboy in suburbia, the anxious worship of no-thing.

Society needs educated priest-scholars to provide structure—the intellectual muscle, bone and skin to keep things together. The university is the Establishment's apparatus for training consciousness-contractors. The intellectual ministry of defense. Defense against vision. This statement is not pejorative but a fact about evolutionary function. We need stability. We need expansion. The far-out vision-ary. The academic council which sits in learned judgment on Soc-rates, Galileo, Bacon, Columbus, Thoreau. The protagonists in these dramas are neither good nor evil. No villains, no heroes. They just are.[15]

So Leary decided to throw in his lot with the "far-out visionaries" of expansion, traded rat mazes and electric grids of conformity ("stability") for the ecstasy of inner space, and taught the youth of the sixties—those unable to connect with the sterile cuckoo religious formulas of the established church—a new creed: "Turn on, Tune in, Drop out." Coleridge's laudanum, his "counterfeit infinity," which lifted him out of his English cottage in Nether-Stowey and bid him drink the milk of paradise in Xanadu, became the sacrament of a new American religiosity, with "Lucy in the Sky with Diamonds" as its anthem, and *Hair* as its passion drama.

This was to be a new age, an age of exploding possibilities for being alive, a dawning age where warm, human light diffused the darkness ushered in by Hiroshima. These children of the Bomb would be the avant-garde of the leisure class, the primogenitors of the psychedelic stone age. Aristotle had said that man was that animal capable of reason, Freud that he was that animal capable of repression, Aquinas that he was capable of faith, Cassirer that he was capable of making symbols, but this was something new and very old—as old as the Sibylline oracles, as the cults of Mother Earth, as the Dionysian festivals. This was the age of Aquarius and Leary wanted to be its priest. Man, he said, is that animal which is capable of *ecstasy*.

With the moon in the seventh house and Jupiter aligned with Mars, the tribe in *Hair* celebrated the "mind's true liberation" from Texas' own Middle American man. LBJ went out to Fourth Street, USA. And what did he see?

The youth of America on LSD [16]

It is gone now, this "new age," this fragile and frenzied moment in the history of the sixties symbolized by the Haight, gone into diaspora. The drug traffic, the Mafia, the panicked citizenry, the inability of the "tribes" to laugh at themselves, destroyed it. Perhaps it would have died anyway, like the beat scene at old North Beach in the fifties. And like Jack Kerouac's and Jack Nicholson's endless odysseys on the road, perhaps the present diffusion of communal life-styles into Utah, Colorado, New Mexico, and Hawaii are destined for the same sadness. Or a new, more politically wise, more theologically sound, rebirth.

Leary went to jail. And then, preferring not to spend the rest of his life there, allowed the militant Weathermen branch of the SDS to spirit him off to Algeria, where he and his wife, Rosemary, joined with Black Panther refugee Eldridge Cleaver. In order to increase Leary's *political* potential, Cleaver placed both of them under house arrest, denying them access to any drugs.

How superbly ironic that two revolutionaries, both for freedom, both exiles from a country they claim usurps that freedom, were set at such odds that one incarcerates the other! The issue beyond freedom apparently is when to take it away.

But for a little while there seemed to be Camelot in Middle-Earth, a put-on paradise. The hippie dream was a utopian vision, a secularization of mysticism. It was a sacramental movement deprived of an ordained priesthood, a protest deprived of a blueprint, a theophany without discipline, a mass movement for utter individuals.

Dr. Leary never became St. Timothy, though Ferlinghetti did call him a priest. His importance lies in his credentialed (within the system) call for "internal freedom," a phrase he used in his last address to a college audience before dropping out of Harvard (with some slight assistance from above). LSD opened up worlds that could never close again, no matter how repressive the system became. William Blake's "doors of perception" had been entered, and like Toyland's borders there could be no return.

When Leary knocked at Allen Ginsberg's door in New York in 1961 to invite him to Boston to guide the new experimental community in psychedelics, he thought that their experiments would be welcomed as scholarly and perfectly reasonable pursuits—even accepted as part of the curriculum at Harvard. Ginsberg recalled later:

Like Leary couldn't conceive of meeting any academic opposition. I kept saying, "You have no idea what you're going to meet, what you're up against," but he was already thinking in terms of, "We'll turn on Schlesinger and then we'll turn on Kennedy"—in terms like that. So I wanted to calm him down a little. . . .[17]

Leary's calm grew less and less, until the day of his manifesto to the students at Central Washington State in Ellensberg, April, 1963.

> So there you have it. I'm sure that a few or none of you will follow the advice and the prophetic warnings that I have been giving. I have had to tell you with words. But I'm going to take my own advice. I'm dropping out of the university and educational setup. I'm breaking the habit. I hope in the coming years as you drift into somnambulance that some of you will remember our meeting this morning and will break your addiction to the system. I'll be waiting for you.[18]

He's still waiting, though slightly more inaccessible.

2

Emptying: Walpurgisnacht
for the Bourgeoisie

Lyrical illusion, nostalgia and adventurism, manipulation. These are
the terms in which the right has exorcized the revolutionary demons
now that the May danger is over; they are too virulent to be examined
face to face. Besides, they are now free, in the name of France's in-
domitable spirit, and by virtue of an enlightened nationalism, to draw
glory from these people, "light, brilliant . . . always consistent with
itself, even in its sudden reversals."

On the left, however, exploitation, canalization, reinflation, count-
ing chickens, too.

And once more the procession of conformisms and calculations of
every kind are reassembled around the old slogans. The whole social
tartuffery, caught for a moment in the trap of naked truth, would
rather integrate the challenge than try to understand it.

HERVÉ BOURGES
The French Student Revolt

Is this what freedom is? Below me, the gardens go limply down to-
wards the city, and a house rises up from each garden. I see the ocean,
heavy, motionless, I see Bouville. It is a lovely day.

I am free: there is absolutely no more reason for living, all the ones
I have tried have given way and I can't imagine any more of them. I
am still fairly young. I still have enough strength to start again. But
do I have to start again? How much, in the strongest of my terrors,
my disgusts, I had counted on Anny to save me I realized only now.

49

My past is dead. The Marquis de Rollebon is dead, Anny came back only to take all hope away. I am alone in this white, garden-rimmed street. Alone and free. But this freedom is rather like death.

JEAN-PAUL SARTRE
Nausea

He listened for a voice of his own, listened, finally, for the neutral, clear, amoral voice achieved most flawlessly by Camus . . .

MICHAEL NOVAK
The Experience of Nothingness

Invocation from Algeria

It was portentous and a thing of state, Vachel Lindsay might have reported, that Leary and Cleaver should have found sanctuary of sorts in the home city of Albert Camus. In the year that Albert Schweitzer went to Lambaréné to become a saint of our century, a boy was born in Mondovi (near Algiers), Algeria, destined to become one of the most sensitive consciences of our century. In Schweitzer was incarnated the struggle of nineteenth-century man to understand and transform his world. In Albert Camus was incarnated the agony of twentieth-century man as he sought to live affirmatively in his world without understanding and without hope of transformation. So Africa received a benediction and brought forth an invocation.

Camus is uniquely instructive for deepening our inquiry into this modern quest for full humanness. Bettina Aptheker, a leader with Mario Savio of the FSM and whose father is one of the leading Marxist intellectuals in this country, in an address entitled "The College Revolutionary's Quest for Values," revealed the intimate relationship between modern Marxism, existentialism, and the supposed "student subversive." The "subversive," according to Miss Aptheker, appears not unlike the liberal Christian, or the sensitive loyal young American who saw her beloved land turned into a desert miscalled "peace" (Tacitus). She concluded with this prophetic estimate of the student revolution:

> The student revolt is not a temporary phenomenon, nor is it limited to a few campuses. Until the central conflicts discussed here

of the university, of racism and of aggressive wars by the United States, are resolved, the revolt will continue and it will spread.

She went on to suggest that central to the protest movement was the agonized desire to be human, to be missional, to believe again that life had meaning. Her concluding quotation was a kind of "subversive" doxology.

As Albert Camus wrote in *The Rebel,* "with rebellion awareness is born." Awareness of being human—of being more than an aspiring carpenter, merchant, lawyer, educator, military officer or dutiful son or daughter. "In our daily trials rebellion plays the same role as does the 'cogito' in the realm of thought: it is the first piece of evidence. But this evidence lures the individual from this solitude. It founds its first value on the whole human race. I rebel . . . therefore we exist." [1]

Robert McAfee Brown, Stanford's remarkably popular professor of religion, vigorous opponent from the beginning of our war in Indochina, and defender of the student liberation movement, calls Camus' philosophy the single strongest alternative we have to Christianity.

I think Brown is wrong. I believe Camus *is* a Christian: a sensuous man who said No to "transcendence" and Yes to freedom. An excursus into Camus' thought may support this contention and suggest his connection with both the activist and hippie dimensions of the freedom movement.

What is man? Camus answers that he is a being who exists in a world without discernible meaning, or rather more precisely, without inherent meaning. The primordial myth of man is not the Garden of Eden as Adam, but the King of Corinth as Sisyphus, condemned by the gods to roll a stone up a huge hill only at each approach to the summit to have the stone roll to the bottom again. There is absolutely no prepared purpose in existence at all. The universe is totally indifferent to whatever we do. We are like sailors on the Zuider Zee, a setting quite unlike the clean air delineating the Grecian isles, where clear deliberate reason sprang fully alive to discipline man's civilizing motion.

But the Zuider Zee is a dead sea, or almost. With its flat shores, lost in the fog, there's no saying where it begins or ends. So we are steaming along without any landmark; we can't gauge our speed. We are making progress and yet nothing is changing. It's not navigation but dreaming.[2]

It is a "stupid" world, a world "hopelessly cut off" from cosmic direction, a kingdom of exiles (*sic!*), alienated in a land without the possibility of music. It is therefore an "absurd" world, hard and grating (*absurdus*), tending to death (*surdus*). So an absurd universe is a tuneless universe, a tone-deaf world where there can be no dancing for joy.

And the guarantee of absurdity is death.

There is no theme which haunts Camus more than the sheer vulnerability of every and any man to death. Sisyphus, after all, was condemned for attempting to chain death. The plague will finally kill you no matter how you fight it, or deny it, or postpone it. Dr. Rieux ends his chronicle of victory over the plague with searing, medicinal honesty. He remembered that the tale could not be one of final victory.

And indeed, as he listened to the tides of joy rising from the town, Rieux remembered that such joy is always imperiled. He knew what those jubilant crowds did not know but could have learned from books: that the plague bacilla never dies or disappears for good; that it can lie dormant for years and years in furniture and linen-chests; that it bides its time in bedrooms, cellars, trunks, and book-shelves; and that perhaps the day would come again when, for the bane and enlightening of men, it would rouse up its rats again and send them forth to die in a happy city.[3]

In a little story translated both as "Cross Purposes" and "The Misunderstanding," Camus immortalized the irrational wastefulness of death. A young husband decides to return home unannounced and disguised in order to surprise his wife and mother whom he had not seen in many years. They have been running a boardinghouse and have decided to murder and rob the next guest so that they might obtain enough money to travel to the young husband. Before the "guest" can declare his identity, he is killed: brutalized between caprice and silence.

The plot of this savage whimsy is planted in *The Stranger* as a newspaper clipping which Meursault finds in his cell, a kind of footnote documenting absurdity. So the "stranger" too is crushed by contingency. Even the literary style incarnates this absence of subjectivity. All causal links are avoided, since they would introduce the germ of an *explanation,* some *order* other than simple necessity or pure succession.

Meursault causes nothing to happen. The sun *heats* him, the *light* blinds him, his *mother's death* disrupts his work schedule, his *woman* makes love to him, his *friend* gives him a gun, the *gun* goes off, the *bullet* kills the Arab, the *court* tries him, the priest *comforts* him. Only here in the last scene does Meursault show passion— when he refuses the comfort of another world and the certainties of the man of God.

> I hurled insults at him, I told him not to waste his rotten prayers on
> me; it was better to burn than to disappear. I'd taken him by the
> neckband of his cassock, and, in a sort of ecstasy of joy and rage, I
> poured out on him all the thoughts that had been simmering in my
> brain. He seemed so cocksure, you see. And yet none of his cer-
> tainties was worth one strand of a woman's hair.[4]

Why this outburst? Because the stranger is a kind of inverted evangelist, a prophet of lassitude, of the final impotence. "Nothing, nothing had the least importance." For men who think they choose are at last chosen inexorably by death.

There is only one final act worthy of a man: to remain lucid to what the sun of nature has revealed—"the benign indifference of the universe."

Camus' problem is quite blankly this: to continue this lucidity and at the same time to cease being an outsider to his own world. His tentative solution is a double negative. He will say no to God and he will say no to death. He will say no to the absolute and he will say no to the dissolution. Man must revolt metaphysically and biologically.

Camus does not really proclaim the death of God. Rather he

refuses God—in a profound sense is angry at God—for the transcendent God of the "Christians" is too far removed from the world to be part of us. And even when the "Christian" God participates he glories in suffering and canonizes death! In *The Rebel* Camus quotes Nietzsche with favor: "If we fail to find grandeur in God, we find it nowhere; it must be denied or created." This means saying no to God means saying yes to the world in a way that makes the world the only truth.

This risk of cosmic defiance is never forgotten by Camus. He refuses "the vast consolation" of ultimate will, the paradoxical adventuring of Kierkegaard's leap of faith, or the final magnetism of Pascal's wager. In fact he reverses Pascal by betting *against* God. "Living," he says, "is keep the absurd alive. Keeping it alive is, above all, contemplating it."

God, then, for Camus is an evasion of absurdity, what Sartre called in *Being and Nothingness* "bad faith," a kind of cheating. If God is alive, he lives in the midst of incredible suffering which apparently he can do nothing about. Ivan Karamazov (whom Camus played on the stage of the Algerian Theater of Travail) faced this inexorable logic of belief, and simply turned in his ticket to heaven. That forfeiture should leave both Ivan and Albert at the mercy of the logic of unbelief—namely violence, ruthlessness, and terror. Camus would reply that nothing is gained by bringing to life a powerless God, and very much could be lost—such as the drive to act now to alleviate the sufferings of mankind through specifically *human* motion. If God for Camus is in some sense still a *deus ex machina,* then I would contend that nearly all popular theistic belief also has this kind of God in mind: a God that alleviates our anxiety about death, powerlessness, insignificance, alienation, sexual guilt, and responsibility. Even a hard-core philosophical theologian like Schubert Ogden (University of Chicago), still defends God as a cosmic memory bank where deeds are stored— God as Dixieland if you please, a "Mind" of cotton where old times are not forgotten: God the Grandfather Almighty.

Camus will have none of this buffering (sounds like a pain-killing drug!). The clean, spare style of his fiction is the perfect setting for his absolute refusal to be anything but aware. Awareness means being vulnerable to irrationality, possibilities of order, hate, hope, meaninglessness, and above all, compassion. Such savage honesty in revolt is precisely what has called forth the observation by Marshall Fishwick commenting on men like Camus:

> No writers have taken fewer wooden nickels in an age of cultural counterfeiting. They have warned us against inauthentic existence. . . . They attack the education of adjustment that presses life into neat packages and crushes into clichés. They know man is a bad actor, full of bad faith. Frequently he refuses to face up to his freedom; hides behind banalities; dodges responsibilities. Like the dishonest dentist, modern man makes a comfortable living disguising decay.[5]

Assurances are born of naïvete says Camus. Father Paneloux, the Jesuit priest in the plague-struck city of Oran, can preach truth with a capital *T* only because he is still in his library instead of on the streets. The nerve of the cultural revolution we are witnessing is precisely here: it is a movement out of insulation and onto the streets where life is not ideological but scabrously raw. Contact with death robs us of certainty and introduces perpetual anxiety. But Camus insists that we must not escape—into alcohol, vocational treadmills, evening charades, or epicurean delights. We must struggle against death with "all our might," "without raising our eyes toward this heaven where He sits in silence." *The Plague* is a sustained, almost faultless, plea to continue the "mad revolt" against suffering, pain, and death. So in *The Rebel* Camus opens his philosophy of rebellion with a passage from Hölderlin (*The Death of Empedocles*):

> And openly I pledge my heart to the grave and suffering land, and often in the consecrated night, I promised to love her faithfully until death, unafraid, and with the heavy burden of fatality, and never to despise a single one of her enigmas. Thus did I join myself to her with a mortal cord.[6]

What is a rebel? "A man who says no, but whose refusal does not imply a renunciation. He is also a man who says yes, from the moment he makes his first gesture of rebellion."[7] What is man as a rebel now? He is Prometheus bringing fires from heaven, the fire of freedom, responsibility, dignity. He is saying yes by saying no, and realizing that his only reward is chains and torture and derision. Yet even hell itself cannot forever hold Prometheus. Perhaps it is our task to create history, not to end it. Out of our frustration, out of the night of death, solitude and estrangement, may yet come a precious, if tenuous, union with the mystery of being. The rebel refuses resignation. He will not allow his life to be mutilated in the name of money, or politics, or religion. The root of Camus' ethics is not a finely reasoned nihilism. His no is a fierce yes—a yes with militant coloring. In almost bemused fashion Camus noted:

> If someone had told me to write a book on morality, it would have a hundred pages, and ninety-nine would be blank. On the last page I should write, "I recognize only one duty, and that is to love." And as far as everything else is concerned I say no.[8]

A vanished beauty, he said, will arise out of our tortured past, the image of harmonious insurrection which bears witness to the greatness of humanity.

One might be led to think that if God did not exist, everything would be permissible. That is what Dostoevski says and he is quoted by both Sartre and Camus. But Camus will not allow the word *freedom* to be perverted into either license or anarchy. Having found the irrationality of life, modeled it on the myth of Sisyphus and personified it in Meursault, having declared war on chaos and capriciousness, modeled on the myth of Prometheus and personified in Dr. Rieux, now Camus drives home the radical judgment of freedom, models it on the myth of Nemesis and personifies it in Jean-Baptiste Clamence. Nemesis was the goddess of moderation and symbolized the limit of perpetual change. She became the "implacable enemy of immoderation." But Nemesis was also justice and retribution, calling all our freedoms before the bar and judging them in the cold light of responsibility. Nemesis in *The Fall* is now called Jean-Baptiste.

We meet him in a small bar in Amsterdam and gradually his story unfolds. He had been a lawyer in Paris specializing in "noble causes" (widows, orphans: pure religion and undefiled!). He helped people, he tells us, a proper humanitarian.

But one evening he heard a laugh behind him and no one was there. It came to him as the laughter of judgment. As he examined his soul he began to see he was bursting with vanity. "I-I-I is the refrain of my whole life." Even in his love affairs he couldn't really give himself. He was a spectator to his own love life! He confesses that once when walking over a bridge on the Seine he saw a woman lean over, heard her fall, but did not attempt to rescue her. His world from that moment on caved in on him. "The whole universe began to laugh at me." He tried to escape through debauchery, travel, but no country was far enough for him to escape himself. He became a "judge-penitent" indulging in public confession at every opportunity, not to secure his own innocence, but rather to implicate all of humanity in his guilt. "Then imperceptibly I pass from the 'I' to the 'we.' "

A *triple trick* has been played on us. First we have suddenly seen that Amsterdam's canals are the concentric circles of Dante's hell, that we have been led inside a Dutch heaven of the last judgment, and that John the Baptist has laid the ax of confession to the root of our vanity.

Our vanity, our fall, our original sin, consisted precisely in supposing that freedom could be handled glibly, if at all. Says Jean-Baptiste:

> Once upon a time, I was always talking of freedom. At breakfast I used to spread it on my toast. I used to chew it all day long, and in company my breath was delightfully redolent of freedom. With that key word I would bludgeon whoever contradicted me; I made it serve my desires and my power. . . . I didn't know that freedom is not a reward or a decoration that is celebrated with champagne. . . . Oh no! It's a chore . . . and a long-distance race, quite solitary and very exhausting.[9]

Radical freedom is a burden, a judgment where we are alone in a forbidding room.

> At the end of all freedom is a court sentence; that's why freedom is too heavy to bear, especially when you're down with a fever, or are distressed, or love nobody.[10]

The trick is *double,* for not only had Jean-Baptiste drawn us into his confession, he has once again refused to take responsibility for himself by the very subtle act of implicating us in his failure!

This deviously shattering statement, this *duplicitus de profundis* in Camus, leaves us at the nadir of self-assertion. Can we really live in a world where "God has gone out of style"? John the Baptist may convict us, but who shall convert us? If there is no transcendent God, and we are locked out of the creeds of assurance from yesterday, is there a possibility of a true humanity?

Yet the trick is *triple.* For while Camus takes seriously the problem of responsibility even while satirizing Sartre's café confessionals, he never really hints at making peace with the "Christian" doctrine of sin. Even admitting that man is tangled in a web of guilt is not the fulsome, the final, the awful point. Freedom as judgment applies most scathingly to God himself. Any John the Baptist is crying in the wilderness not to see this, and the Christian church according to Camus is full of false prophets. In *The Fall* he plants that excruciating paragraph asking about the melancholy air hanging over the Gospels. That brooding quality is the result of guilt—not man's but God's: the God of Jesus that slaughtered the innocents so that the Bethlehem babe might live, a Messiah by murder. God has watched the martyrs die, the wars of religion rage, the inquisitor's flame consume. If God is, *he* is responsible, if not as actual perpetrator, then as, in Peter Berger's phrase, "eternal bystander."

Richard Rubinstein, the Jewish "death of God" theologian, is totally immersed in Camus on this point, and shifts from the New to the Old Testament this somber criticism—no, too weak a phrase, this "agony of insight." The reason, Rubinstein says, that no Jews after the crematoriums could believe in God is *exactly* because of their heritage as "the chosen people." This assumption of uniqueness has forced them through the centuries into unimaginable deprivation and persecution. *After Auschwitz* Israel's faithful arrogance is impossible.

So it is that Camus' challenge through *The Fall* is almost the reverse of the historic one thrown out by Voltaire. It is not the whimsical "If God did not exist, we should have to invent him," but the scathing "If God did exist, we should have to destroy him."

The Fall was originally to have been included in the collection *Exile and The Kingdom,* but developed beyond the appropriate length for that book of short stories. One story in particular in that collection suggests the central contradiction between freedom and social authority. It is called "The Artist at Work."

A painter, Gilbert Jonas, is swallowed up (what else!) by conditions around him: his wife and three noisy children (*sic*), his tiny apartment, and his early success as an artist. Jonas retreats into his bedroom for some privacy. The phone rings, the children scream, the wife goads, and he cannot work. At last he builds himself a loft and climbs into it. There in a feverish fit he works in the dark, painting his "masterpiece," finished just as he collapses. A friend climbs the loft and discovers a completely blank canvas in the center of which Jonas had written, in very small letters, a word which could not be made out with any certainty. The friend could not tell whether it was "solitary" or "solidary."

The "artist," then, is metaphor for the most profound split in our culture between the values of individual freedom and necessary community. These values both compete and complement. They are in what Roszak would call "the dialectic of liberation." We are solitary in the inexorable demand to be ourselves, but that uniqueness finds itself always revealed within the compromise of community.

Freedom, therefore, is an ellipse with two foci: I and us (solitude and solidary). The "artist" is schizoid only when he stops the rhythm of the dialectic on either pole. This is why it is crucial for us to pass through the death of God. "God" as "transcendent authority" adds a third element to the ellipse—or rather, *over* the ellipse. This God distracts, deflects our attention from the dialectic, and in fact promises a relationship abstracted *from* the world of self, other self, and other. Such certainties *are* not worth one strand of any artist's hair.

A Time of Axial Man

It seems clear to me now that the period from the end of World War II to the beginning of the sixties allowed cultural permeation of this "death of God." To speak of political or social rebellion without speaking also of spiritual rebellion is to miss the heart of freedom itself. This is why Albert Camus was so important to that permeation. He did not merely dismiss God as an unnecessary obstacle in the path of human progress, or an incidental deflection of attention (not prayers, but plows, said Marx). He *hated* "God." It is that hatred, that religious awareness of the seriousness of the human condition, the illuminating occasion of divine absence, which is the price we must pay for being modern Christians.

Camus was awarded the Nobel Prize for literature in 1958, cited by the committee as the man who had most illumined "the problems of human conscience in our times." His own absurd death in a sports car crash, January 3, 1960, exactly opened our decade: a bizarre invitation to Walpurgisnacht.

The early sixties became the *kairos,* the right time, when the fact of "God's death" surfaced with popular finality. Karl Jaspers, the German existentialist philosopher, has called the eighth to the sixth century B.C. the time of "axial man," a period so pregnant with meaning that history seemed to cry for a breakthrough: the prophets in Israel, the Buddha in India, Lao-Tze in China, the golden age in Greece.[11] Perhaps the sixties will become known as Walpurgisnacht for the Western world, the age when authority died, the exorcism of "God": Robinson in England, Bloch in Germany, Sartre in France, Altizer in America. Whatever collection of serious religious thinkers we bring together we must be impressed by the extraordinary cohesion between radical freedom and radical theology, between our awareness of the emptiness of death and the fullness of life.

I have called Camus a Christian, in spite of his own professed leanings toward Taoism—and the "Greek Spirit"—and have spent some time developing his interpretation of freedom. This is not mere academic license. The fact is that we do not know what Christian faith is until we are driven by some event to face the final caprice of this multiverse. It is impossible to speculate exactly what this event might be in the life of any given person; for some of course it would be a series of moments, or for others immersion in an art form. But I submit that such an event took place for

Americans in the death of John F. Kennedy. This suggestion needs some explanation.

Twenty-seven hundred years ago, in the time of "axial man," there lived in tiny Judah a powerful king named Uzziah. Empowered by popular approval, impassioned warriors, and great riches, he represented the zenith of government in that little land. His reign was long and prosperous and his people, we are told, felt secure under his leadership. He was a religious man and kept near him in Jerusalem royal prophets for consultation concerning the will of God. His very name meant "God is my might."

One such royal prophet was named Isaiah, a young man of sixteen, an aristocrat, whose confidence in the future of Judah was inspired by his devotion to Uzziah the king. Uzziah's virile, wise, and merciful government inspired Israel to dream of the day when Uzziah would restore Judah to the glory that was David's Israel.

Then one day, the dream was shattered. Stricken with the dread disease of leprosy, Uzziah died.

The old securities were shaken, and young Isaiah, fearful and sorrowful, went into the temple to pray. It was to be the most significant day of his life, for it was on that day that the revelation came to him. In the chaos of governmental transition, in the unmerited sufferings of a royal friend, in the crumbling fortunes of national sovereignty, in the stark terror of the unknown, in the face of final silence of the grave—in *that* day, in *that* time, divine vision came to Isaiah: "In the year that King Uzziah died, I saw the Lord. . . ."

On a crisp fall day in 1963, from a sixth-story window in Dallas, Texas, a shot was fired that exploded the back of John F. Kennedy's skull. In one awful, agonizing, demented moment, a dream was shattered and a nation plunged into darkness at noon. And like Isaiah, many of us, in fear and disbelief and inexpressible sorrow, entered into the temple to pray. Our words might well have been uttered in anguish in the eighth century before the Jesus-Christ-event. Isaiah spoke for America:

> The whole head is sick
> and the whole heart faint,

> From the sole of the foot even to the head,
>   there is no soundness in it,
>   but bruises and sores
>   and bleeding wounds . . .
>
> How the faithful city
>   has become a harlot,
>   she who was full of justice!
> Righteousness lodged in her,
>   but now murderers.[12]

In such a day as this, can we "see the Lord?"

The truth is that it is *only* on ominous autumn days that we *can* see. Our lives apparently are organized around the principles of survival and self-perpetuation, and this means that it is possible to construct rational models in manipulating the processes of those lives. All science is based on this fact: that the "universe" will support our systematic, disciplined investigation of its operation. As Harlow Shapley, the famed Harvard astronomer, put it in *Of Stars and Men,* "All is in fact orderly; . . . Chaos is but unperceived order." [13]

This assumes a tentative inexorable character intrinsic to our phenomenological models. Objects heavier than air fall to earth. If the law of gravity were suddenly repealed so that sometimes those objects flew up, we should have to alter the model. A necessary postulate of our modern life is the orderliness of nature. A bullet fired from a $12.98 rifle, if aimed properly, will kill even the President of the most powerful nation on earth, and "God" will do exactly nothing about it.

Theologically speaking, to assert the unity and reliability of the natural process is to affirm monotheism. We recite creeds affirming *one* God, Almighty, who created *this kind* of world in the light of "his infinite wisdom" as to what kinds of worlds were possible. So physicist Robert Millikan once said that no scientist could be an atheist, for he could not by *definition* believe that *chance* operates our universe.

Even as a believer, therefore, I remain a rational man. As a rational man I am forced to see that all kings must die. The world is so ordered. No man or king or president will endure forever.

Some constellation of circumstances will consign each to death. John Wesley speaks plainly to this point in his seldom read *Advice to a Soldier:*

> Death levels all: it mingles in a dust the gentleman, soldier, clown, and beggar; it makes all distinctions void. When life ends, so do they.[14]

It is this theological affirmation about the integrity of life and death that was underscored with such bitter irony by the parable of two graves in that searing autumn. Two men: both dying of gunshot wounds in the same hospital, both buried on the same day, both leaving behind a widow and two small children. Gentleman . . . and beggar! Death levels all.

Suddenly our entire nation was confronted by the fact that God will make no exceptions to his order—no hidden shields protect us, no special invulnerability surrounds us. To put it cosmically: nails tear the flesh of the son of God as well as the sons of men.

This address to inexorability has a powerful inversion as its strange corollary. If God has so limited (leveled) the world by his creation, he has also within those limits set that world free. E. E. Aubrey commented in *Patterns of Faith in America Today* that man was the only creature with an *if* in his vocabulary. Carl Michaelson said it in a much more specifically American way: "God has turned the world over to men." Much of what we call "evil" can be attributed to the fact that amid inverted orderliness of nature man may choose to be disorderly. He is free to love or to hate, free to shield or to shoot. And this freedom is so *radical* that it will not be abrogated by environment, legislated by government, or even dissipated by disuse.

As we have seen, the political philosophers through the centuries have struggled to hammer out a policy which would allow full recognition of man's freedom without disintegrating into absolute license. In this sense, even the limitation of freedom by the government is only legitimate in the name of *natural rights* of all men. Our nation is a great experiment dedicated, at least in writing, to this basic proposition: that everyone has the "innate" privilege to liberty in life. And our nation has always explicitly recognized that "God" is the guarantor of this proposition. From the Mayflower

Compact, to the Declaration of Independence, to the Pledge of Allegiance, to the minting of our money, the affirmation is bold and unmistakable. We are a covenant people—under "God."

Our political freedom therefore is grounded in what we take to be the will of God: that he had made us free, and this divine dignity is bestowed in full recognition of both its privilege and its problem.

The privilege is that we might rise above the level of sheer instinct to full self-consciousness and personhood. We are granted, so we think, the glory of *using,* instead of *being,* machines, of having relationship instead of merely being related. The rhetoric on this line is interminable, but the privilege is real. We will not become puppets with graciousness. *Never again* says the Jewish Defense League.

The problem is theological. For the tree in the paradise of personhood bears both good and evil fruit, both destiny and danger. Our freedom means that "God" is a gentleman and does not come in where he is not asked! *It means on a deeper level something much more stunning: importuned or no, he does not come in.* Bergman's *Winter Light* captures this realization in somber shades of gathering dark. Pastor Tomas, ineffectual as either man or minister, confesses to a disturbed fisherman who has sought him out for some hint of solace in this bleak world:

> I became a clergyman and believed in God. (*Gives a short laugh*) An improbable, entirely private, fatherly god. Who loved mankind, of course, but most of all me. . . . A god who guaranteed me every imaginable security. Against the fear of death. Against fear of life. A god I'd suggested myself into believing in, a god I'd borrowed from various quarters, fabricated with my own hands. D'you understand, Jonas? What a monstrous mistake I'd made? Can you realize what a bad priest must come of such a spoilt, shut-in, anxious wretch as me? [15]

Alone a few moments later, he cries out in anguish: "God, my God, why have you abandoned me?" Then the full force of his confession tears open his heart: "God does not exist any more . . . I'm free now. At last, free." [16]

This is what it means to identify Kennedy's death as an event of caprice that drives us into the possibility of faith, what it means to use orderliness models in science as confessions of human freedom, what it really means to proclaim "in God we trust": GOD HAS TURNED THE WORLD OVER TO MEN. Jerusalem is destroyed by pagan powers and God does nothing. The ovens at Buchenwald are hot with human flesh and God does nothing. The jungles of the East are red with blood and God does nothing. The mighty and the unremembered fall, the widows weep, the children stand mute with misunderstanding, and God does nothing.

> O Lord, how long shall I cry for help,
>   and thou wilt not hear?
> Or cry to thee "Violence!"
>   and thou wilt not save?
> Why dost thou make me see wrongs
>   and look upon trouble?
> Destruction and violence are before me;
>   strife and contention arise.
> So law is slacked
>   and justice never goes forth.
> For the wicked surround the righteous. . . .[17]

In the year the king died, I saw the Lord.

Infinitely Untraceable Calls

This, I think, expresses what so many of us felt that late November day in 1963. And at that very moment college students everywhere were reading the words of Dietrich Bonhoeffer, the brilliant young German theologian, martyred by the Nazis in 1945, words made internationally famous by their quotation in Robinson's *Honest to God.*

> God is teaching us that we must live as men who can get along very well without him. The God who is with us is the God who forsakes us (Mark 13:34). . . . God allows himself to be edged out of the world and on to the cross. God is weak and powerless in the world, and that is exactly the way, the only way, in which he can be with us and help us. . . . Man's religiosity makes him look in his distress

to the power of God in the world. . . . The Bible however directs him to the powerlessness and suffering of God; only a suffering God can help.[18]

These were not the trivial musings of a lonely and desperate political prisoner, as Karl Barth once suggested. This is the central affirmation of faith for the Christian. In "God" we trust means we are mortal. One nation under "God" means that we are quite free to allow utterly stupid men to destroy everything we hold precious.

This understanding of the religious situation of the last half of the twentieth century has been building like a great ocean swell that starts far out at sea, gradually generating enough power to rise, curl, and pound the shores of our cultural psyche. It began with the Jesus-Christ-event, surged forward onto the reef of the Renaissance, until we ourselves were caught in the wave of empirical freedom which washed our whole society clean from the "God hypothesis." Creation started it; Jesus called the Christ illumined it; Copernicus and Galileo proved it; Darwin, Marx, and Freud exposed it; Nietzsche announced it; Frazer and Malinowski systematized it; Franklin Baumer documented it; Camus personified it—and Dietrich Bonhoeffer baptized it.

There is no longer any need for God as a working hypothesis, whether in morals, politics, or science. Nor is there any need for such a God in religion or philosophy. In the name of intellectual honesty these working hypotheses should be dropped.[19]

Bonhoeffer, like most of us, had some nostalgia for the old *working* God, the God who somehow *arranges* the flow of history and corrects any misdirection of that flow. He remembered a song: "It's a long way back to the land of childhood. But if only I knew the way!" But there *isn't* any such way, and Bonhoeffer himself has become a kind of saint of secularity, cited, lauded, and almost canonized by such contemporary voices as John Robinson, Paul van Buren, and Harvey Cox. And it was William Hamilton, self-elected president of the "death of God" school, who suggested the volume of essays published as *The Place of Bonhoeffer.* Our situation is simply that when the "universe" becomes a puzzle instead

of a mystery, then "God" as an explanation may be dropped with
no more than this twinge of nostalgia. I, too, remember a song:

> Toyland, Toyland, little boy and girl land,
> While you dwell within it you are ever happy there.
>
> Childhood, Childland, mystic fairy Toyland,
> Once you pass its borders you can ne'er return again.

It is worth noting that the "death of God" theologians came out
of our universities, surfaced after Kennedy's assassination, and developed contemporaneously with the student revolt, the civil rights
struggle, and the escalation of the Vietnam war. The cohesive fac-
tor between the "death of God" and the "movement" is that they
are both wars of liberation, and in some very rich sense are inter-
dependent.

This relationship would appear to be very tenuous, if not fatu-
ous. Black power, brown power, student power, are readily con-
nected, and even organized as a Third World Coalition at the San
Francisco State struggle. But death of God theology has seemed
remote and esoteric. It is not. It is my thesis that Benjamin's
"transcendent" freedom *is* God's death that locks the church, and
gets the bus (read revolution) moving.

Now "death of God" may still seem contradictory to many,
rather like "hot ice." But there are very many different meanings
of the phrase. Martin Buber translates it as "the eclipse of God"
(*our* problem, not God's!). Hamilton likes the neat epigram: "the
experience of the absence of God, not the absence of the experience
of God." All common garden-variety ministers think that God has
been neglected and, if dead, passed on from disuse (read: collec-
tions are down). Paul van Buren continues to make up his mind
about the function of the letters G-O-D, and earlier insisted that the
word "God" was dead.

However, the interpretation that really deepens our understanding and anoints my celebration can be stated with deceptive simplicity: *the death of God means that God is Being.* Students of
Paul Tillich will immediately add "Itself" to "Being" and Altizer

fans will begin to feel twinges of *satori* around the edge of their anxieties.

It will be no surprise to sophisticated readers (is anybody still there?) that Tillich must be included in death of God theology. He stated flatly that God does not exist:

> God does not exist. He is being-itself beyond essence and existence. Therefore, to argue that God exists is to deny him.[20]

And further (Tillich always gives us a "further"):

> Thus the question of the existence of God can be neither asked, nor answered. . . . It is as atheistic to affirm the existence of God as to deny it.[21]

Now what Tillich meant, obviously, was that God is not a thing, an object among objects, even the *highest* or *biggest* object, but the Ground of all existing things—with "religion" consequently that sphere which interpenetrates all other spheres. Tillich was an "ontologist" (the essence of the cosmos is "being") and said frankly that to ask about God's existence is to betray that fact that you are not asking about *God* at all. God is dead when suffocated by arguments *about* him. God (for heaven sakes!) is the presupposition of God!

Such an interpretation seemed persuasive to Robinson and "pop Tillich" became a runaway best seller. Tillich came as emancipatory good news to a whole generation of college students who jammed his lectures and attempted to appropriate the "courage to be." It was more than warmth that caused Thomas Altizer and William Hamilton to dedicate their book *Radical Theology and the Death of God* to the memory of Paul Tillich. While Altizer publicly acknowledged his debt to Tillich, he also sought a model for selfhood in Eastern mysticism, almost becoming self-consciously a kind of Christian Buddhist. His first book was entitled *Oriental Mysticism and Biblical Eschatology,* and he revealed his double background when he insisted that the doctrine of God was the Emperor's Clothes of modern theology. He would, as he said, expose the nakedness of our theologians—in fact the nakedness of all men before the void.

> The confession of the death of God is now the price the Christian must pay for contemporaneity.[22]

But what is this "death of God"?

> Wherever we turn in our destiny, we are confronted by the nothing: for the Death of God has been followed by the resurrection of the Nothing; the Nothing is now openly manifest in the deepest expressions of contemporary existence.[23]

This is that death: the final affirmation that God is No-Thing, that he is energy, motion, awareness, a "movement of being," a "radical immanence." This is both that death *and* the appearance in fullness of "the face of God."

Altizer has distinguished himself from Tillich's "eschatological pantheism" (God is *in* the world but is not exhausted *by* the world) by calling his own thought "dynamic pantheism." This "pantheism" Altizer illustrated by reference to a remarkable trinity: Paul, Hegel, and William Blake! The central metaphor is Paul's use of the word *kenosis* (Greek for "self-emptying") to describe the incarnation. God, who was transcendent creator, *emptied* himself into the world in Jesus, and thus died into being-in-the-world. To put it rather crudely, it is as if God bored a hole into the world in order to pour himself into and permeate his own creation. So Altizer spoke fondly of Hegel's "kenosis of eternal Being," and even more fondly (one might say ecstatically!) of Blake's mysticism.

> With the death of God, a primordial Being existing in itself as its own creation or ground has been shattered, and with its dissolution every alien other loses its intrinsic ground.[24]

Thus the "body of Christ" is the dead God who is now the Being of the world, or as Blake puts it in cryptic contradiction: "The Eternal Great Humanity Divine."

In this way Altizer moved from immersion in mysticism to a

clear-toned "gospel of Christian atheism," and has continued on to "descend into hell"—to study what he now calls a "radical reversal of the Christian Consciousness." Heaven and Hell are obviously symbolic categories, he reminds us. Heaven is most naturally the symbol of the transcendent realm, something distant and beyond, evocative of the bliss over urfreedom, disorder, and suffering. Hell then is not unheavenly. It is rather its direct and intrinsic opposite, the radically immanent realm of freedom, chaos, and death. Hell is precisely to be understood as *the center of the earth*. This is not a crude, primitive spatiality, but profound *Christian* imagery:

> Hell is the underworld, it is "below" the earth; or, more truly understood, it is the embodiment or center of the chaos, the darkness, the turbulence, and the pain of earth.[25]

Our convocation of witness grows. We are called away from the heavens to listen only for those voices likely to speak. Lawrence Ferlinghetti's poet's eye obscenely sees what Thomas Altizer's mystical mind obscurely sketches, what Franz Kafka's tortured imagination grotesquely spins.

> Kafka's Castle stands above the world
> like a last bastille
> of the Mystery of Existence
> Its blind approaches baffle us
> Steep paths
> plunge nowhere from it
> Roads radiate into air
> like the labyrinth wires
> of a telephone central
> thru which all calls are
> Infinitely untraceable*

Things That Go Bump in the Night

"Christian atheism" is not, as all citizens of Coats, Kansas, would agree, a persuasive phrase, but it points in the right direc-

* Lawrence Ferlinghetti, *A Coney Island of the Mind.* Copyright © 1958 by Lawrence Ferlinghetti. Reprinted by permission of New Directions Publishing Corporation.

tion for the act of faith. What it communicates is the vital clue that we must not start with any concept of God other than the idea that God *is* the world, that his very being is our life. Paul van Buren, becoming lucid after his "ontological hangover," speaks with power to this point. What is God? Van Buren answers that God is the possibility, not of the anonymous, mobile, secular city, but of the banyanlike polyverse "ancient city." In an address entitled "The God of Imagination" he said:

> God is that which allows everything in the city to be just exactly what it is, the rain falling on the just as well as on the unjust. God is that which sees everything in the ancient city just as it is. Not a sparrow drops to the ground without notice. As for the realization of God's full authority over the city, in that hour, it will be in the city, just as things are now. A seed dropping by the wayside, people being invited to dinner and most not bothering to take what is presented, the opportunities of life before us which a few grasp and most ignore. And what did the teller of the parable have to say about this, for the life which, in fact, we all lead? He had this to say. That this is all real, indeed, the only reality there is, that the taking or ignoring of these opportunities is not trivia, not preliminary, not secondary, but final. That who we are in such situations is who we are for good.
>
> This ancient city cannot be put in parentheses as preliminary, tentative—only a dress rehearsal for a later "real performance" which transcends it. To be ready for the kingdom means to start living now, in the present.

We *all* live in "this ancient city" and to be a "religious" man in that city means to me to have both a vision and a celebration. That is, the religious man asks two questions about his city: How do I see life? and Can I embrace what I see? The first is *word;* the second is *worship.* The first *perspective;* the second *participation.*

Proper Christian vision cannot begin with "God." It starts with "man" and his experience of what it means to be a man. It ranges over the heritage of competing visions of true humanity and identifies Jesus called the Christ as teacher, exemplar, and incarnational hero. He is found in the "ghetto" of the city (that succession of instances which defines specifically who we are in our uniqueness), but already in being found he is finding—and breaking down the walls that divide men from themselves. He is a *free man,* with that quality of caring, of increasing sensitivity to the needs of individuals and community of self-affirming integrity and self-giving, opening up to the possibility of true human relationship. And, above all, the Christian does not demand divine *imprimatur* before he sees life in this manner. If death of God thinkers have taught us anything, they have taught us that no such demand could possibly be met. The resurrected Christ, I would remind culture Christians, never appeared to any except those who loved the living· Jesus. "Death of God" as an intellectual fad has long since faded but the full force of that movement continues to break in on us. We are now in a counterpoint of religiosity and neopietism (the "Jesus freak" genre) which will intensify concurrently with our fascist tendencies. But the "damage"—the deed of liberation—has been done. We will enter 2001, if at all, without metaphysical warranty. The "psychedelic stone age," the requirements of Aquarius, demand a new, almost electric integrity.

It was to this Christian, this radical responsibility, that we were called in the sixties by Edward Albee's *Who's Afraid of Virginia Woolf?,* another excruciating vision of the human problem and a brutal call to celebration. Here Albee intruded with ferocity on the last citadels of our ease.

Two faculty couples (the elder in the history department, the younger in the biology department) meet at 2 A.M. in an after-party on Sunday morning near the campus of New Carthage College. After fun and games of increasing virulence ("humiliate the host," "get the guests," "hump the hostess"), in the very witches' hour (Walpurgisnacht), George and Martha (the older hosts), tempted to the edge of self-exposure by their own competitive ferocity, "bring up baby," an imaginary child dreamed up over the years to insulate them from their own sterility. In a final exorcism, George "kills" the son, torturing Martha with his capricious and satirical power over the "boy's" existence, alternately inventing absurd circumstances for death (the "boy" crashed into a tree avoiding a porcupine) and chanting the consolations of Christendom:

Libera me, Domine, de morte aeterna,
in die illa tremenda: Quando caeli
movendi sunt et terra: Dum veneris
judicare saeculum per ignem. . . .
Requiem aeternam dona eis, Domine: . . .

As the requiem mass is intoned against the ritual of Martha's
desperation, Nick—recalling the very first words of the play—
begins to see what the evening is all about. "Jesus Christ, I think
I understand this," he says very quietly. Then, almost as if we
might have missed the full force of his own revelation, he repeats
violently:

JESUS CHRIST, I THINK I UNDERSTAND THIS!

Do culture Christians really understand? Think of the inner logic
of human selfhood. There was a time when men of wisdom defended the body only as the encasement of the soul. And in re-
covering for the body a rightful place of honor, some became
utterly foolish, reducing human life to barren sensuality. So we are
constrained to reaffirm the unity of body and soul: the one world
of humanness. The self discovers the mirror of introspection.

We taste—from strident, infantile suckling to adult voracity. We
react to odor, disguise its unpleasantness, create aphrodisiac moments with it, release a flood of memories—and realize we are a
collation of odors: illusory, erotic, and nostalgic. We begin life by
being touched, embraced, and no amount of maturity ever quite
robs us of that primitive desire to be held and to hold, to know the
texture, the temperature, the shape of experience.

We photograph our environment and in the transfer of images
seek to delineate the visual cues from the reality which the cues
introduce. We are bombarded by vibrations ranging in frequency
from utter silence to intense silence, and in between we convolute
audibility into communication.

But none of these senses by themselves, or altogether, constitute
humanness. There is another fundamental element, a kind of sixth
sense, a peculiarly human phenomenon that galvanizes the five
senses. It plays under many names; now it is called laughter, then

it is called language, in academia it is called reason, in the market-place common sense, in philosophy abstraction, in religion transcendence.

It is in fact the ability to symbol—to allow one thing to stand in place of another, to objectify experience, to be aware of the self as distinguishable, if not separate, from the rest of reality.

It is to this symboling, subjectivizing self that men of wisdom have given the name "soul." And it is precisely because we possess this capacity for awareness of the self that we have tended to resist any identification of the soul with the body. Since the soul is our uniqueness, then it must be primary, even the whole of pure humanity. It may even survive the dissolution of the body and have a life of its own. A life of its own without the senses would demand a new spiritual body and a place for continued awareness. Thus images of angelic beings and heavenly places were conjured up and passed on as canonical articles of faith.

Our traditional Easter further bids us touch and taste the spiritual body of the risen Christ, smell incense symboling the presence of the Spirit, see the beatific vision where we have shuffled off this mortal coil, like a chrysalis bursting the cocoon of flesh, and hear the angelic choirs:

> Made like Him, like Him we rise, Alleluia,
> Ours the cross, the grave, the skies, Alleluia.

The miseries of earth's toil and suffering are over—hallelujah! It is a glorious faith, is it not?

It is just this faith that is called into question by Albee. The senses have been honored in deteriorated communion, fun and games in New Carthage, humanities and sciences in mortal combat. What better symbol of the intimacy with the senses than a biologist? What better advocate of abstraction than a historian! Yet for all his sensuality Nick is impotent when his image of himself is challenged by Mother Earth. And for all his expertise in human events, George is sterile when it comes to producing life in that same Earth.

Then all of them—Nick, George, and the Great Mother—exploit

that peculiar human ability of distinguishing idea from reality. They insulate themselves from who they really are by the device of sheer illusion. Nick would understand himself as a creature of the laboratory, insulating himself from dreams and romance by raw statistics. George would understand life as devoid of statistical measure, insulating himself and Martha from evidence by dreams and contrived romance.

But now the hour of darkness has come. It is night and New Carthage has fallen. It is black Friday, Nick a truculent Satan, George a sainted clergyman intoning the requiem mass. And the queen mother: "through her soul and anguish groaning, bowed in sorrow, sighing, moaning, past the sharp and piercing sword."

Liberame Domine, de morte aeterna, in die illa tremenda. . . .
It is Walpurgisnacht, the witches' hour, all the demons out to haunt us, to shriek out our weakness, our utter folly at dividing body from soul, mind from spirit, all the frenzied spirits loose now to torment us with exposure of ourselves, our careful constructions of who we are.

Now, it is time in New Carthage—the Son, the only begotten Son, the illusion that protects us from being truly human, that perverts our humanness into filters against wholeness, *that* Son must be killed: crucified, dead and buried.

Liberame Domine, de morte aeterna, in die illa tremenda. . . .
We must stand before life naked, anxious, but authentic, freed to be ourselves in communion with a world of other selves, justified not with special knowledge of the path ahead, or of the meaning of the next step. But—if you will allow it—*justified by faith alone.*

Jesus Christ, I think I understand this now.
JESUS CHRIST, I THINK I UNDERSTAND HIM NOW!

3

Deciding:
The Eschatological Hero

Traditionally, eschatology has taken the form of an expectation of the future transcendence of the human condition for all mankind in inexorably advancing history. And it is against this expectation, whether in the form of Biblical eschatology, enlightenment, progressivism, or the theories of Marx and Hegel, that modern "psychological" critics have taken their largely conservative stand. But not all eschatological theories are theories of history. There is another kind of eschatology, which might be called the eschatology of immanence.

SUSAN SONTAG
Against Interpretation

Today we find ourselves caught in a moral dilemma: unable to accept the destructive conformities of patriotism, national honor, authoritarian religion, yet wary of the old poetry of alienation with its overtones of self-punishment and isolation. The love-ins and be-ins of the past few years may well express this disarray. They show dramatically how many of us today are groping toward some new language, some new heresy.

PAUL ZWEIG
The Heresy of Self-Love

If only I could lead him out of his emptiness, away from his life-god. If we could dare to show each other tenderness. If we could believe in a truth. . . . If we could believe . . .

MARTA IN BERGMAN'S
Winter Light

From Superman to Superstar

The mosaic formed in this confessional—epigraphs as connectives between artistic witness, argument, and personal event—is now plainly emerging as the classic Christian way of salvation. But a major impediment to experiencing this mosaic remains. Our problem is that the Christian story has come to be identified with the American myth. They are not the same. The American myth calls us into the future by driving us into the past. It attempts to insure freedom by emphasizing law. It preaches individuality by placing redemption outside man himself. America has been nourished on a hero mentality, a sports charisma, celluloid illusions, and political star systems. It is absolutely correct culturally that our most recent President should have been raised in southern California, scattered accolades to athletic power, and courted the spiritual benediction of both Billy Graham and Norman Vincent Peale.

I grew up on heroes. We all did. My first memories were of Buck Jones, Hopalong Cassidy, and Jack Armstrong. Once a week my grandmother took me to the old-time serials: the Shadow who knew that the weed of evil bore bitter fruit, the Lone Ranger and the glorious days of yesteryear, a group of intrepid horsemen called the Three Mesquiteers—and there were Tarzan and Jungle Jim.

My father was a hero—a shortstop who hit over four hundred in a Midwestern baseball league and was sent a contract by the St. Louis Cardinals. So were my brothers—football, debate, theater and various valedictions—and I began to build my fantasies out of their achievements. One day—it was in June of 1938—a brand-new hero entered my life through *Action Comics*.

Born on the planet Krypton of renowned scientist parents Jon-El and Laura, this hero was named Kal-El, and escaped the complete destruction of his planet by means of a rocket predirected toward earth. The rocket landed near Smallville, U.S.A. (later reports indicated that it was nearer Johnson City, Texas) and there he was found by John and Martha Kent and named Clark. This little child soon displayed his otherworldly powers by deflecting a speeding train from its track and leaping tall buildings at a single bound.

After an adolescence free of both nascent sexual tension and acne, Clark Kent journeyed to Metropolis, that great city, and took a job as a reporter on the *Daily Planet*. He acquired a semi-girlfriend named Lois Lane. At ten years of age I thought Lois Lane totally unnecessary, and even more so another early girlfriend named Lois LaMaris, who it turned out couldn't really get serious—since she was actually a mermaid and had the singular disadvantage, not fully appreciated by me then, of being all scales from hip to tail.

It was in Metropolis that Clark Kent donned the red cape, the blue tights, the shirt to show the torso that was more-so, and on his sternum emblazoned the crimson *S*. Thus had he come to save us, to make all my other heroes seem vulnerable. The Shadow had to cloud men's minds, Jack Armstrong ate Wheaties, the Lone Ranger wore a mask, my bothers were interested in women, and my father had even married one, but *this* was a man of steel! Faster than a speeding bullet, more powerful than a charging locomotive: Look up in the sky—it's a bird, it's a plane—it's Superman! And, by God, it was.

Then one day I met him again, not in the comic pages, but on the lips of a charismatic clergyman. He told me of a strange man whose origin was mysterious and far away and whose young miraculous life was entrusted to peasant parents in a small village in Palestine. As a youth he restrained his powers, but as a man he entered his vocation of fighting for righteousness, by turning water into wine. He walked on water, healed the sick, calmed the storm, made the blind to see, and when at last he was killed, he came back alive as before and floated far out into space from whence he had come. Look up in the sky. Is it a man? Is it a Messiah? No—it's Super-Jesus! And by God it was.

Crude and naïve as it sounds, this Jesus Christ, Superstar image is still with us, preached lasciviously, sung erotically, and defended with some sophistication in theology. David Jenkins, chaplain to Christ Church College in Oxford, author of a *Guide to the Debate About God,* was asked at an international conference of Methodist theologians if he believed that Jesus was raised bodily from the grave. His "instant-humble" reply: "Well, I wouldn't put it past God!"

Chad Walsh, poet and professor of literature at Beloit College, was for many years an agnostic. He recovered his "transcendence" (*Stop Looking, and Listen*) and took on the nation's arrogant sophomores in his wry collegiate credo, *Campus Gods on Trial*. His most remarkable defense of the faith was also an attack on "scientism" (the position that scientific "law" exhibits a closed universe).

Once upon a time, said Walsh, there was a Martian who was very "scientific." He came to earth in this little flying saucer and "observed" the phenomenon of city traffic. He noticed—Martians were extremely precise—that certain moving objects (cars) were stopped in flight by lights that were red. They moved ahead on green. Since he recorded this identical phenomenon in several cities (to allow for the variables) and many times (to allow for chance), he concluded—Martians were very bright—that *red* stops cars, while *green* makes them go. Back on Mars, contented scientists wrote "earthen traffic laws" into their books, and lived on in positivistic bliss.

Then, one day, that same Martian, conducting a field trip for his students at Mars State, saw a shattering sight. A *car,* with lights flashing on top and shrieking with splitting sound, went flying right *through* a *red* light. My God! A miracle: natural law broken right before their own antennae!

Now as a parable of modern physics and eighteenth-century British empiricism, this story is right on target: there are no *laws* but only statistical probabilities. But Walsh then—it's really in the book—uses it to support the Biblical miracles as actual historical occurrences.

Usually men don't see waters divide so that they can walk across on dry land, but when Moses and the Israelites came to the Red Sea, it was an emergency. Lights flashed, sirens sounded, and the waters were swept away. *It was God going through all the red lights!* [1]

Those awful Romans and stiff-necked Jews had nailed Jesus to the cross, thinking they would do him harm. Now he is laid in a dark tomb and shut off forever by death. But wait. Thunder, lightning, earthquakes, rocks rolling back. It's God again—just in the nick of time, zapping the world with that old red-light emergency.

Super-Jesus! Son of Mandrake! When the drama of salvation must go on, there is Jesus Christ, Superstar.

I understand the need for this, for the periodic eruption of the "Jesus freaks," bubbling up through the caldron of disintegrating value systems. As long as that interface is here between technological advance and inquiry into the perspectives informing that advance, the fault of fascism will move, will tear. The agony of that movement will tempt us into messianic copouts. Now, especially, when the entire superstructure of Western history is on the verge of disintegration, when radical freedom is finally emerging for keeps from Christendom, we can expect one last great effort by "Christian fascists" to keep us in place. Call it a swing to the right, to the middle, a rebirth of liberalism, a return of religion or to law and order, it is all motivated by a nostalgia for authority, a final refusal to be free.

Look at the example of our century. It opened after four shattering revolutions in Europe. Darwin put man in his place in the hierarchy of evolving animals; Marx put "God" in his place, using Hegel to systematize man's alienation; Freud "reduced" man to subconscious forces of self-preservation and procreation and showed man's religious life as fatal illusion; Strauss "reduced" sacred scripture to sequential scraps of mythic musings.

Is it any wonder that Friedrich Nietzsche felt justified in pronouncing quite openly (1882) in the name of Zarathustra that the base of Western culture had collapsed? A madman rushed into the marketplace—today he would scarcely be noticed—and cried out:

> I seek God . . . Where is God gone? I mean to tell you! We have killed him—you and I! . . . God is dead! . . . The holiest and the mightiest that the world has hitherto possessed has bled to death under our knife,—who will wipe the blood from us? [2]

Thus we came to this century, not really despairing at our lack of light, or weeping at the funeral of God, for most did not realize he was gone. We had our reason, and science was a new Messiah. We would soon put wheels on our feet, wings on our back, and fling words around the world. If there was no heaven with streets of gold, at least this world could be golden.

In 1914 this dream of the golden age of man was shaken by World War I. In 1939 it was crushed by Hitler's legions marching into Czechoslovakia. The century of progress had become the century of horror. In 1945 the *Enola Gay* spread a mushroom cloud over Hiroshima, and with it extinguished the last light man possessed.

Where could he go for help to build a new world? What could keep him from cursing the darkness? He could neither go back to the light of the authoritarian church of the thirteenth century, nor to the light of revealing scriptures of the sixteenth cenury. He could not now go back to the light of easy reason of the eighteenth century. Where could he go?

Somehow we had to continue the vision of graceful and orderly empire which Wendell Willkie had called "one world," for when the specter of Nazi supermen crushing Europe aroused the world of ordinary men to human heroism, it was the men who won and not the supermen. All nations would soon unite in the age-old dream of the Parliament of Man. Then at last on the East River in New York, nations would learn war no more and beat their swords into plowshares. In the Security Council an artist painted the hope of the world: The Phoenix rising from the ashes of destruction.

But were we really the victors, we men of flesh and blood and weakness? Perhaps we were a nation of destiny still, a nation made strong by a power not ourselves. After all, our national anthem and our money proclaimed our faith, and on every field of battle we had a chaplain. So we added that phrase to the pledge of allegiance: this nation, "under God." Our people flocked back to church, the highest crest of attendance and membership in the history of America. Evangelists and clergymen flooded the land, packing football stadiums, calling us back to our knees. The grace of God has saved us. It is our only hope. "The Bible says," shouted a tall, wavy-haired North Carolinian, a Wheaton College graduate: "Blessed is the nation whose God is the Lord, who has led us through the wilderness of war and by his strong right hand has gotten us the victory." He used—of course he used—the image of the Super-Jesus: the invulnerable man of salvation who cannot be defeated, with his virile arms, his flashing hair, his X-ray eyes that peer inexorably into the soul of the world, the mighty one of God! Yes, Virginia, there is a Messiah.

It is an irresistible temptation, an almost involuntary historical reflex, to speak this way—not limited to attractive ecclesiastics. Who among us escapes this temptation? If God appears dead to the careful "modern" technician, there is always a mysterious monolith just out yonder beyond the stars. A few majestic chords from Richard Strauss' *Also Sprach Zarathustra* and there we are past the tool-perceiving apes into the outer reaches of the universe, waltzing to the moon, discovering the great ebony monolith, conversing with a conscious, willful computer named HAL (IBM), rocketing into Jupiter on the good ship *Discovery,* millions of miles from earth: a reclining psychedelic eruption into everywhere.

Let Pauline Kael, the brilliant, vitriolic film critic (*I Lost It at the Movies*), return us to earth:

> . . . *2001* is a celebration of cop-out. It says man is just a tiny
> nothing on the stairway to paradise, something better is coming, and
> it's all out of your hands anyway. There's an intelligence out there
> in space controlling your destiny from ape to angel, so just follow
> the slab. Drop up.[3]

And she continues relentlessly to hold us on the point. This is a grand plan which "justifies slaughter and ends with resurrection" and promises that we "can go to heaven in Cinerama."

Such a reflex to escape this earth, however sophisticated, is a direct denial of our true heritage of freedom in Jesus called the Christ. When we follow the cross instead of the slab, we drop everything.

And How Do You Like Your Blue-eyed Boy Now, Mister Death?

We are ready now to offer an alternative to the "transcendent" authoritarian God of Christendom, and a precise explanation of just why it is that this "God" is not Christian. I think it is quite clear that without such an alternative we are likely to enter the new age spiritually impoverished and unable to consummate the movement already begun in the colleges, the Third World liberation coalitions, and the hippie dream. Already the promise of that age is compromised because no central myth has grown up to provide the ritual of cohesion.

The most attractive formulation of this alternative has been made by my former teacher, Joseph Mathews, the charismatic man who troubled Albion, and has organized a remarkable revolutionary cadre to "renew the church." Mathews has never published, except for an infrequent article (his "The Time My Father Died" is something of a classic), and his kerygmatic work is found only in mimeographed form used by the staff of his organization, the Ecumenical Institute.

Ironically, he too has been labeled a "Christian fascist" and an intellectual fundamentalist. But Mathews is neither. His is the most powerful voice in the Christian community today calling us to "pick up our lives," decide to be who we are, and throw ourselves into the "breach of history." He entitles the theology of this call: "The Christ of History."

Mathews begins by reminding us that men everywhere have needed to make sense out of our human action. That need has entered our literature as *Everyman,* the dream of final blessedness, a power of deliverance that will enable us to really live in this world. Under the urgency of this need, people everywhere forge symbols to celebrate that hope. The ancient Hebrews called their peculiar symbol story the *Messiah,* the coming anointed one, translated into the Greek as *Christ.*

The *Messiah* symbol, the *Christ* symbol, is born in any historical people (any culture that assumes the historical process itself to be potentially meaningful) of a sense of limit, the experience of finitude, what Tillich often spoke of as "the ontological shock": that moment in history when we know that we will cease to be, when we come up against the indifference of the universe and our insecurities are exposed. These anxieties are the breeding ground of the Christ symbol, as the finite creature strives relentlessly to escape his insignificance. That creature dreams of another world, for this world of the now is far too threatening, far too burdensome, far too final. Surely out there somewhere is emancipation and fulfillment.

Men dwell sometimes very explicitly, most times quite vaguely, in great expectation of that which will relieve them of the necessity of living their given life in the present situation. This great hope, whatever its form, is the CHRIST OF EVERYMAN.

The attraction of the Super-Jesus image, the transcendent God-figure, becomes perfectly clear as we begin to understand our own primordial hopes. John Updike changed the name of Everyman to Rabbit Angstrom, but his disguise is all the more frightening. An "angstrom" after all is an absolutely minute measure of a light wave (one hundred-millionth of a centimeter), as well as being a play on the German word for "fear." So we seek out heroes, authority figures, coaches, clergy, whores. And when we fail to freeze life into high school games, fail to assuage our anguish in fatherhood or fornication, we run and run and run. It is only a question of time before someone asks in desperation: "Are you running with me, Jesus?"

The New Testament opens with a specific historical people expecting the Messiah: Christ. Mathews insists that this concrete occasion must not be reduced to an abstraction. It was Joshua of Nazareth, translated Jesus, who intruded into the Jewish yearning. It could have been "Herman of Hebronville, or Jones of Smithville." But it was not. It was Joshua: Jesus.

This specific man lived and died, as all men do. Yet his life was what Mathews calls a "plus," had what Whitehead would have termed "the elucidatory power of special occasions," or Ernst Fuchs "a speech event" quality. Jesus apparently really *lived* his life, appropriated it as an unqualified gift and understood himself as having "cosmic permission" for his very presence in history.

The very point is that Jesus collided with the lives of all he encountered. He invaded, broke into, penetrated their worlds, leaving them painfully unsettled. To the proud he seemed humble and they were threatened. If men hated life, he loved it. To those who hung desperately onto living, he appeared nonchalant about it all. If they thought of life as detachment, he was utterly involved. If their living was a bondage, he was too obviously free. Where men were other-directed, he was independent. When they were confidently self-determining, he seemed lost in loyalties. To conservatives he was manifestly revolutionary; he impressed the radicals as a reactionary. Obviously, the life of such a human being would be in jeopardy. When men's lives are audited to the quick, either they must re-do their lives, or destroy the occasion of the audit. Jesus was executed.

All men must die. But this man was killed because somehow in his living he exhibited the very meaning of his own life. These are the few facts that we know about Jesus. As Albert Outler turned it epigrammatically: We know precious little about this man Jesus, but the little we know is precious.

In the midst of this Jesus-happening, says Mathews, some individuals were grasped by a radically new possibility for living, and these few men raised the blasphemous suggestion that he might be the *Christ*. Some raised it directly as a question: "Are you the Christ?" This question reveals a double intention and it is, in Mathews' vocabulary, the "key to the Christ-happening": *scandal* and *decision*.

The scandal is absolutely clear. *Everyman-Christ* is a mighty King, a Davidic Warrior, a cosmic figure who would fulfill the dreams of Israel, reestablish the lost Kingdom, overthrow the tyranny of Rome. Jesus was born a helpless baby in a manger trough. He was a common carpenter's apprentice in a shabby Palestinian village. He strangled to death on a state gallows. *Messiah? Christ?* It was indeed a fundamental offense to the Jews to suggest such a thing. They were quite right in labeling it blasphemy.

Now we are moving closer to the heart of the "scandal," for the offense of the Jews is the offense of *Everyman*. It is a question of human self-perception: we know ourselves in Jesus-Christ, not to be in the future, but in the present. The meaning of life is not to be sought after in some quest; it is given in the now. The Jesus-Christ language puts it bluntly: "The Kingdom of Heaven is at hand." All men who look to tomorrow to give significance to today, who attempt to escape the present as meaningless, will be outraged at the intimation that ultimate meaning is *only* present in our very concrete situation. This is the scandal in the question: "Is Jesus the Christ?"

Do not miss this understanding. If Joshua: Jesus is to be called by the symbol *Messiah: Christ,* then some radical inversion of that Christ symbol has taken place. The most fundamental dream of man has been shattered, a total image disputed: *the Messianic Hope has been stood on its head!*

As Mathews puts it: "The *Jesus-Christ* mortally assaults the *Everyman-Christ."* It is this victorious assault which crowns the scandal and allows us to grasp the drama of human decision.

> The JESUS-CHRIST fronts man with the awareness that there is no Messiah and never will be one, and furthermore, that this very reality is the Messiah. This must not, however, be understood as an intellectual abstraction. It is rather a happening, that meets men in the midst of their living. Indeed the fronting is experienced as death itself. For to receive the *Jesus-Christ* is to put an end to my Christ quest; it is to surrender my very life stance; it means that I must die to my very self. Or better still, my self must die. The threat of the JESUS-CHRIST is now unmasked as the threat of death. The Scandal, as experienced, is that I must choose to die.

To be seized by the scandal of the Christ-happening is to be plunged into the arena of decision. The New Testament drama, the Jesus-Christ-Event, is permeated by a double decision: the *Jesus-Christ* who picked up his own life, who chose to die his own death, and the *Everyman,* who is outrageously faced with this deciding man, and who therefore must decide who he is, and by deciding, become fully human himself.

To put it quickly: Jesus-Christ exposes us as creatures of sheer existence, and forces us to declare whether we will affirm life or negate it. There is *no* middle ground here, no place for retrenchment, for insulation from the shock of choosing. Either you are for us or against us. Either you say yes to life or no. We embrace or we reject.

The New Testament writers underlined this stark and final dichotomy of deciding with a marvelous richness of figures: light versus darkness, God versus Satan, angels versus demons, Heaven versus Hell, life versus death. What we sometimes fail to see, in our crass misuse of these figures, is that they are all informed by the key figure of *crucifixion* as prior to resurrection. When Paul says that without the resurrection we have no hope, he could be translated as saying that the decision to give up our illusions is to embrace our exposure. So final (and painful) is this decision that we can only compare it with death. But to die in this way is to live as Jesus-Christ. It is, as the gospel of John puts it, like being born all over again, like being blinded in order to see, like the healing of a paralyzed body, like a resurrection from a tomb.

Our resurrection then only proceeds through our crucifixion, and is the seal of our embrace of that death. That is, we live *in* our anxieties, learn *in* our ignorances, affirm *in* our negations, and find freedom *in* our historical limits. We choose in darkness to walk not because this choice will *diffuse* the darkness, but because we *must* walk. The light is in the choice to walk. In the Christ-myth of *The Graduate,* Mrs. Robinson is Satan only so long as Benjamin allows himself to be done to rather than to do. Even when he takes up his cross she does not cease to be Satan, any more than the world ceases to be world in the Christ-story. The God-image in the Christ inversion means that all the Mrs. Robinsons, Everyman everywhere, remain in history as the very occasion for making history.

Let Mathews summarize this alternative understanding of the Christian faith:

> Now to the recapitulation: the JESUS-CHRIST is an historical event. It is a radical revolution in the interior history of men proceeding from an absolute reversal in human self-understanding. Originally occasioned by Jesus of Nazareth, it is first of all the experience of an offense. This offense is grounded in an actual disaffirmation of our creaturely phantasms which issues in a new possibility of living our bestowed existence as a great benefaction. It is secondly, the decision to receive the offense and embrace the ensuing possibility as our now. This entails a dying to ourselves as defined by our mirages, which very death is experienced as the very life we were mistakenly searching for. Such is the radical transfiguration of the JESUS-CHRIST-EVENT.

We are not quite through with our understanding of intentionality as bodied forth in the Christ-happening. In order to complete the picture we must re-create both the Christian Story and the Cultic Christian Man.

The Christian Play

Every people draw out life apologues, meaning stories which freight their self-understanding, great narratives like *El Cid, Beowulf,* the adventures of the angel Moroni, the epic of Gilgamesh, the *Iliad,* the Exodus from Egypt, the winning of the West. Liturgy is shorthand for these stories, and it would be a serious mistake to conclude that our present American culture does not need either a liturgy or a narrative. A major part of the rootlessness and desperation of our time—one of the reasons for the new nostalgia, the neo-pietism in the Jesus movement, the turn to the East and the quest in astrology and tarot cards—is the need for awesome, definitive, cosmic drama. The Christian Story—aesthetic theology—is a powerful and persuasive myth, and, appropriately told, might still fulfill that need.

This Christian Play is a tale of two symbols: the cross and the empty tomb. The leading character, as Mathews sees, is not Jesus at all, but "the bi-form symbol, cross and open sepulcher."

. . . Once the story is devised, there is a certain absolute quality about even the form. In principle, the detail could have been quite different at its creation. And any time thereafter, its basic intent can be expressed in other ways. But once the original dramaturgy is complete, that production is the prototype. It remains prototypal as long as the historical community remains.

The play has two stages (upper: transcendent; lower: historical), and three acts. The first and third acts are similar—with a decisive difference. Both take place on the upper stage. In the first—in the beginning of beginnings—the *Jesus-Christ-Event* is disguised as curious lamb on a throne, slain, yet alive, creator of all things. The third act again places the lamb, alive-while-dead, on the throne as King of Kings, this time judge of all things. It is the ending of endings. The lamb is the First and the Last, the Creator and the Consummator. The Church's liturgies reenact them as *Pater* and *Spiritus*.

Act Two is embraced by two transitional scenes, whose theatrical function is to get the lamb on and off the lower (historical) stage. The *Jesus-Christ-Event* is heralded by angels, born of a virgin, and worshipped by wise men. Thus the "virgin birth" is a theatrical device, which has nothing to do with evading the messy intimacy of copulation. This is not biology, but theology—a restrained, gentle, and altogether lovely introit to the earthly pageant.

So too when his "history" ends, he is caught up by clouds of glory to be transported to the throne. Once again, this "ascension" is no miraculous rocket shot to a city four-square floating somewhere fifty miles above the earth, from whence the "risen Lord" will return in astounding ubiquitous style ("every eye shall see him"). This is not aerodynamics, but eschatology—a spatial exit that proclaims the universality of this specific life. For he who grows in Nazareth and dies in Jerusalem is *over* us all. Let the heavens open and let them orchestrate the glories of the lamb, let all creation celebrate this revelation, this Apocalypse: he is Lord of Lords—he is worthy that was slain—and he shall reign forever and ever.

Mathews *might* have included that the promise "he shall come again" is a kind of director's clue that the play will *never* end, but will be repeated every time a human being decides to be present to his or her own historical possibility.

At last, then, we come to a summary of the middle act.

The central character is still the JESUS-CHRIST-EVENT. Camouflaged in the first and last act as the slain lamb, it is here disguised as a man. In this double concealment the cosmic figure submits to the ordeal of finitude. He meets and straightforwardly engages the twin forces of death and the devil: that is, the temptation to illusion and the anxiety of creatureliness which drives us into the clutches of illusion. He engages the forces of EVERYMAN-CHRIST and destroys their power by boldly withstanding their subtlest wiles. He enters the very den of death and emerges from the grave the unchallenged conqueror. In a mighty invasion, the JESUS-CHRIST-EVENT has overcome the hosts of the foe on the plains of history, pushed to the fortified place and bound the strong man, leading humanity forth from its bondage and slavery unto the glorious freedom of life. The sign and power of the cross and empty tomb are engraved for all time upon the face of history. Cosmic permission to live has been epiphanied. Mission accomplished, the lamb returns to that realm from whence he came, the manifest victor to rule as sovereign lord and only judge forever and forever. What a play!

The components of the Christ-construct are now obvious: the Everyman quest, the Joshua-event, the scandalous decision to identify Joshua as the fulfillment of that quest, the radical inversion of the meaning of that identification, the forging of a cosmic drama to invoke the power of that inversion. There remains one more component: the etching of the eschatological hero.

This hero is a far remove from our childish models of derring-do and familial projections. He is the Jesus-Christ-Event as *both* the temporal Jesus *and* the transcendent lamb. On the one hand he is the son of Joseph and Mary, runs the gamut of life's joys and sorrows, and dies. He does not, however, capitulate to the lure of the future redeemer, but elects to embrace his humanness ("I and my Father are one!"). On the other hand, this hero also strolls across the sea of Galilee, turns water into wine, and raises dead men to life. This is not magic, not Super-Jesus, not Martians misreading the ineluctable laws of nature. This is the activity of an archetypical hero on a mission of ultimacy that takes place in actual time.

These two poles (cosmic and human) are blended together with such artistry that the New Testament portrait of Jesus-signified-Christ is awesome in its simplicity. Now he is eating supper, now stilling storms; now embracing little children, now cursing fig trees. The Christian community always recognized that to separate the Jesus-Christ polarity would somehow violate the story. They sought to translate the coalescence into Greek in a series of ecumenical councils, climaxing in A.D. 451 at Chalcedon. It was a mysteriously direct formulation ("both divine and human, unconfusedly and inseparably . . .") and has been singularly ineffective in helping succeeding generations to see the point of the incarnation, to *feel* the power of the "Word made flesh."

Mathews has taken us back behind those obscurities, barbarisms, and metaphysical abstractions to the sheer drama of human decision.

> With utter intentionality, the hero lives as the free man. He humbly opens himself to what is given; gracefully receives himself in what is given. He is liberated to be thankful for life; to love this world of neighbors; to be directed toward the future. This is to say, he is free to live life. And while he is busy living, he simultaneously declares to those about who have ears to hear the good news that they too can live in the freedom of the JESUS-CHRIST-EVENT.

This is the heart of our alternative to "transcendence" and the present imploding crisis of authority, our secular epiphany. There really is no compromise between this Christianity and culture Christendom: either you are for us or against us. And there is no other name under heaven whereby we must be saved, save this Jesus-Christ. We may never have heard the name Joshua: Jesus. We may come out of entirely different cultures, where all the *specific* symbols are changed and the meaning story staged with other players. But once these symbols are decoded or experienced as confessions of faith and their imperatives understood, then we may judge them. Do they call for radical responsibility, or do they not? Do they point us to each other as creatures who tomorrow will not be, for which every moment in this life is as precious as it is precarious, who must wait for no further gift from God but this one and final gift of birth and becoming, who must refuse to surrender our humanness for any cause, and who choose to lay down our lives for all that defines us as open, imaginative, ecstatic flesh?

What do the life apologues say?

Do our own rituals open us up or close us down? The *Jesus-Christ-Event* is light and in it is no darkness at all. It is lucidity, like a sun in the center of mankind. Stand with our backs to that sun and we will look only at our own shadows, dream dreams of other worlds, and weep at our isolation. But the sun goes out, warms, and welcomes, and if we turn around we will not be blinded. We will, for the first time, see each other.

Name it what we will, it is *conversion,* rebirth. It is not an exposé of all the mysteries of existence which will allow forgotten holiness

92   *The Sensuous Christian*

to haunt us in new superstitions of the spirit. It is the embrace of those mysteries—not in order to solve them, but to love them.

I think I *really do* understand Jesus Christ now. The Jesus model is the *Jesus-Christ* made flesh. To walk in his steps is not to imitate Jesus, memorize his words (or print them in red), or even to reproduce his life. To be Christian is to do our truth as free men.

The Feast of Good Jesus

The very last piece of fiction that Camus published lifts up this radical inversion of the Christ symbol and dances with it. It is a moving narrative of intentionality, the Christian play disguised as pagan story, woven with all the threads of resistance, alienation, and decision: Sisyphus as the *Jesus-Christ-Event* celebrating communion in exile.

The story is set in South America, far from either the decadent wrath of Europe or the mystical Eden of Algeria. An engineer named D'Arrast has come to build a dam near the Brazilian town of Iguape and is being honored by the mayor of the city, even to the point of giving him authority over the local chief of police. D'Arrast becomes acquainted with the village native culture through his chauffeur, a native named Socrates. Socrates tells D'Arrast about the local religious holiday, "The Feast of Good Jesus," celebrated because of a miraculous "growing" stone in a grotto, to which the faithful bring hammers to break off a piece for happiness. The night before the "good Jesus" procession the natives dance in a big hut in another feast—this for St. George. D'Arrast meets a stranger at the grotto who has been saved from drowning by good Jesus and promised to carry a hundred-pound stone in the procession. The yellow-skinned stranger, a ship's cook by trade, invites D'Arrast to the big hut for the paroxysmic ritual to St. George, where the cook dances too feverishly and too long, and where D'Arrast is finally asked to leave just as the ceremonial modulations begin to climax. The next day, the cook collapses under the stone before he reaches the church. Then D'Arrast, like Simon of Cyrene, picks up the burden and carries it, not into the church, but back down the trail into the big hut, dumping it among the ashes of the last night's communal orgy. The poor natives gather into a circle around the stone and ask D'Arrast to sit with them. The chiding words of Socrates seem to echo as the circle closes, engineer and peasant (foreign power and native): "In your country there's only the Mass. No one dances."

William Power has reminded us that theology can only be told as a story, and Mathews' paper brilliantly illustrates this. Camus himself said that philosophy can only be written as a novel. Perhaps we might let the case for decisional selfhood rest here, with this final story: Sisyphus in a grotto, engaged in an absurd task for a stranger that still allows the stranger his manhood in fulfilling the task *for himself.* This sensitivity to *spiritual* need, without reliance on miracle or institutionalized faith, this identification with the land, the body, the common circle of humanity—this and nothing else is the kingdom. To eat at the feast of good Jesus is to take the burden of understanding. That alone is the rock that grows, upon which community is built. In the early part of the dance, D'Arrast was asked by the native to unfold his arms: "You are hugging yourself and keeping the saint's spirit from descending."

One *could* make a case for this century as a new axial period of history: Nietzsche's announcement of the full fruition of the renaissance, three world wars (*three*), the technological-humanities interface, the emergence of the Third World, the climax of the reformation, the ecological revolution. The question on every serious mind is raw and desperate: Is this the Apocalypse?

> *Karl Marx* and *Sigmund Freud* together show
> Oppression alternates with Overthrow.
> The proletarian Id combines its mass
> With Superego's castellated class
> To pinch the bourgeois Ego out of power:
> The flag of Anarchy besports a flower;
> The telescopic rifle and the cunt
> Emblazon Urban Youth's united front.
> The world boils over; Ho and Mao and Che
> Blood-red inaugurate a brighter day.
> Apocalypse is in. . . .*

* From *Midpoint and Other Poems* by John Updike. Copyright © 1963, 1969 by John Updike. Reprinted by permission of Alfred A. Knopf, Inc.

On the banks of Manila's river stands a palace belonging to the age of supermen, where some spent nights in five-thousand-dollar beds and Castilian governors reveled with caprice and cruelty. Agnes Newton Keith wrote a novel showing what happened to that palace, and Wallace Hamilton used her description thematically in a series he entitled *The Thunder of Bare Feet.*

> There are fingerprints now on the palace walls, soil marks on the curtains, thick carpets grown thin, souvenirs are taken, garden flowers are picked and green grass trampled on. For two hundred years this palace has flourished while the people had grown thin. Today the people gather strength from the palace. Here they come, barefoot or well shod, ignorant or brilliant, poor or rich, bad or good, old or young.[4]

Hamilton comments that we should keep our eyes on that palace, for it is what we are seeing all over the world: "It's a small snapshot, but of a much larger scene. The many are rising up to be the rulers. The shirtless millions are climbing up to power. The barefoot ones are walking up the steps to the palace."[5]

Not quite the Apocalypse? Then thunder, the thunder of bare feet. Intentional men and women getting loose, picking up their lives, and dying their deaths. This is Vietnam and the People's Republic of China, this is Cuba, this is Watts and Hunters Point, this is Berkeley, Africa, Soledad Brothers, Sister Angela, and the long march to Washington by thousands of the poor. And if we cannot hear it now perhaps we can see it in the sizzling flesh of a young Quaker in front of the Pentagon or a monk in southeast Asia, in the forgotten flash of a draft card, the scattered ashes of a bank near Santa Barbara, the agonized idiocy of a Chicago conspiracy trial, on the balcony of a motel in Memphis, the hot Chicano hovels at Delano, the militant exiles in Algeria, the pathetic addiction to the stars, or—most virulent of all—the final eruption of white suburban captivity.

Or perhaps we can still see it more clearly, more redemptively, on a lonely hill in Jerusalem, where a barefoot man shuddered out his life with a cry, "My God, my God, why have you forsaken me?" A few barefoot men were so seized by the quality of that life and death that they flung around the world a communal story that they were one with him and he with them. It is twenty centuries later and there are still human beings, those who know themselves related to all mankind, who embrace life and death in the face of radical uncertainty, who storm the palace of the mighty and turn out the money-changing supermen—they still walk in his steps. Bishop Stephen Baynes is one of them.

> The Incarnation is really an essay in freedom. . . . Mankind is too much given to weeping over the cross. [Jesus] does not intend that we shall be flabby and precious in our devotion. This is the act of the strongest and freest of men, who freely chooses even this supreme obedience in choosing above all things that the Father's will should be done. This is the Christ of the Gospel—this Person who from the first to last shows no fear of freedom, asks no favors from it, accepts it, uses it, fulfills it. Whether he is alone in the wilderness choosing the manner of his obedience, or in Galilee teaching men how to live within the matrix of their freedom or supremely acting out his freedom in the most final terms of life and death, the impact of Christ is the same. He is, for all humanity which will follow him, the supreme teacher and exemplar of what it is to be free. The life of service which he taught and lived, the standard of tenderness and patience and humility which he showed, the undeviating loyalty and obedience which live at the heart of that life—this is the supreme contribution of the Christian tradition to man's endless conversation about what it is to be a man.[6]

I grew up on heroes, and they are all gone now, all except one, who remains for me both King of Kings and man among men—the Messiah who never comes, yet releases us instead to fill that emptiness with our own decision not to be Messiah, but to be fully human. He was the man who set his face like flint for Jerusalem, who took up his cross and decided who he was. And his life as incarnate freedom is still our life.

This is why I received Benjamin as a man when he picked up the cross. His past was over, his bondage by a world he did not make. This was his world, awakened by richly liking another self, deciding to live out his new being in the capricious present of Morgan Street.

PART II

Love: The Grace
of Sensuousness

If you will go down into yourself, under your surface
    personality
you will find you have a great desire to drink life direct
from the source, not out of bottles and bottled personal
    vessels . . .
The soul's first passion is for sheer life
entering in shocks of truth, unfouled by lies.

D. H. LAWRENCE
From *The Complete Poems of
D. H. Lawrence,* edited by Viv-
ian de Sola Pinto and F. Warren
Roberts. Copyright © 1964,
1971 by Angelo Ravagli and C.
M. Weekley, Executors of the
Estate of Frieda Lawrence Rav-
agli. All rights reserved. Re-
printed by permission of the
Viking Press, Inc.

4

Consuming: The Cost
of Subscribing to *Playboy*

As a sexual cripple, the pestilent character who is endowed with more
than average bio-energetic agility must develop channels to somehow
live out his surplus energy. He will be a master in cunning, slyness,
"know-how" in getting along with people *smoothly*. He will stand out
little from the crowd. He will be a "good fellow," people will like him,
he will appear honest and straight, and he will really mean what he
says subjectively. But he will never overcome the feeling of being an
abortive genius, gifted and crippled at the same time. This is strongly
developed in him, and he has this trait in common with most average
people.

WILHELM REICH
Truth versus Modju

There had been a period in his life when *Time* solemnly took him out
in the backyard every few weeks to give him a going-over—in return
he had never been able to strike back with more than a little rhetoric
on *Time's* iniquity until the mighty occasion when he captured the
mistress of a Potentate of *Time*! That lady, in the final phase of an
extended liaison, had most certainly been on the lookout for the particular sweet fellow who would most outrage her Boss. The Prisoner,
being fresh out of Bellevue, gave money's worth. If, in a story he had
once written called "The Time of Her Life," the protagonist had been
fond of referring to his sexual instrument as The Avenger, now the
Prize-winner whammed nothing less than a Retaliator in and out of
Vengeance Mews (thereby collecting a good share of the poisons the
Potentate had certainly left behind) and was so intent on retribution it

99

took him months to recognize that the dear pudding of a lady in whom he was inserting his fast-rusting barb was a remarkable girl, almost as interesting, complex, Machiavellian, and spiritual as himself. The experience marked him profoundly (to a marriage and one of his children indeed!). He was never again so good a revolutionary—in fact, he ended as a Left Conservative.

NORMAN MAILER
"The Prisoner of Sex"

Behind the ghastly grinning figure of war with its death head and dripping hands, behind the Moloch of commercialism with its brutal claws upon the fluttering wings of life, behind all the cruelty of man to man and man to woman, stands lust—clothed as a woman in gorgeous robes, with bare breasts and a smile beckoning men to follow her.

STUDDERT-KENNEDY
Lies

Up from Methodism

The explosion of intentionality which drives the Christian into his own history and reveals his apocalyptic humanity is only one side of the matter. And in order to develop the other part of the Christian drama we now have to start the play over again, so to speak—retrace our pilgrimage from the perspective of the other side.

The cross is still a highly charged symbol of decision: with its shape of a man on its crossed lines pointing to all parts of the compass, demanding inclusively that we choose our own direction. From the eschatological hero story there follows an eschatology of immanence.

But that same cross has another charge, more potent and thus more zealously hidden. To put it directly: it is also a phallic symbol standing tall against the darkened sky of repression.

This last suggestive imagery of the crucifixion is not particularly recent, for it appears in a book of casual anthropology entitled *The Masculine Cross,* published anonymously in 1891 and is still kept locked up in the Private Case at the British Museum. It is just as well. The Anglican Church is already unhappy enough with Bishop Robinson, and, who knows, libidinous communicants might start thinking of stained-glass windows as surrogate vaginas. In fact, a London biblical scholar, John M. Allegro, has published a book entitled *The Sacred Mushroom and the Cross,* which attempts to prove that the name "Jesus" stems from the Sumerian *ia-u-shu-a,* meaning "semen which saves, restores, heals." The mushroom, according to Allegro, has partial symbolic reference to the female organs, and combined with its obvious chemical properties provides ample range for the imagination. Who knows what he could make of the "rod of Jesse"—not to mention the Johannine ejaculation: "Even so, come, Lord Jesus."

The imagery, though, has zest. Projected onto the freedom myth of *The Graduate,* it converts the scene at Santa Barbara from flaying authority with its sword of the Lord into bolting Calvin with a flying phallus! (How perfectly smashing, as the British would say.) It also allows us to call attention to our most irresistible, revealing, and powerful instrument of rebellion; namely our sexual lives. What happens, of course, is that in developing freedom in advanced, competitive societies we express the first resisting stage sexually as *consumers* of each other, in Norman Mailer's vocabulary: as *cannibals* and not *Christians.*

One of the ironies of our capitalist society is that its health depends on our disease. That is, we must be rendered competitive by the educative system in order to drive forward the production of goods and available services. When this intense competitive *esprit* finds itself empowered by technology, it goes berserk attempting to manufacture a market for its accelerated productions. As that same technology depersonalizes its producers, it sets the mood for a humanizing revolution, but it also introduces the temptation to express that rebellion as a *consumer.* This, I think, is the plain logic of America's so-called sexual revolution, and it is painfully illustrated (embodied?) by the history of *Playboy* Magazine.

Nearly a generation ago a new magazine appeared in America. Its young editor, Hugh Hefner, had just quit a sixty-dollar-a-week job as a copywriter with *Esquire* to launch this enterprise. Mr. Hefner's concept was appropriately direct: to publish a first-rate magazine aimed at the sophisticated young adult male world. His strategy was equally straightforward: to combine literary excellence and perceptive guides to sensual enjoyment.

For eighteen months Hefner struggled along with moderate success. Then in July, 1955, he persuaded Janet Pilgrim, head of his subscription department, to pose for a gatefold nude photo in exchange for an addressograph machine for her department (we can be grateful that she didn't need a computer!). Thus was born "the girl next door" beauty—fresh, clear-eyed, firm young playmate, in marked contrast to the jaded, cheap, whorelike look common to male magazine nudes. *Playboy* had arrived.

Today Hugh Hefner is a multimillionaire, and his mansion in Chicago a mecca for an incredible variety of entertainers, intellectuals, and social revolution leaders. His magazine is easily the most phenomenal publishing event in journalistic history. As I write this, subscription sales are six million, and more readers will lust through *Playboy* this month than will read all the religious magazines, political, cultural, and literary periodicals put together. William Hamilton once called it the "best written, best edited, most consistently interesting magazine in America," and it clearly increased during the sixties in both range and depth. The center for instructing Peace Corps Volunteers at Hilo, Hawaii, required its trainees to read the latest issues in order for them to become aware of their own cultural values before they attempted to understand another culture. *Playboy*'s influence as a tract of our times became so enormous that Hefner, as its mythlike spokesman, was invited to appear on nearly every major campus in America, and reputable campus theologians felt pressured to undertake a serious analysis of his views (Harvey Cox, of course, in *The Secular City,* Richard Hettlinger in *Living With Sex,* Jerome Nielson in the Lutheran Quarterly, *Dialogue,* Benjamin Garrison in *Creeds in Collision*).

In fact, Hefner himself felt this pressure and rather than leave his underlying assumptions just lying around under whatever there is at the Chicago mansion, began to articulate them in an interminable editorial entitled "The Playboy Philosophy." It was his original intention to answer the criticisms of Harvey Cox first published in *Christianity and Crisis* in 1961, but the answer spun out past twenty-five installments and when last heard of was being edited for possible publication as a book.

Hefner's main thesis on which he rang his creedal changes was that a radical readjustment in moral focus was needed in our nation. The new orientation in our ethical ethos should be centered on this proposition: that personal behavior was the individual's business exclusively as long as that behavior did not injure mutual liberty in society. Or as Anson Mount, public affairs manager of *Playboy,* put it in an address entitled "A New Breed of Cat":

> At *Playboy* Magazine we are neither proponents of adultery nor chastity, but what we do believe [is] that your private life has no necessary correlation with whether or not you are a good and useful citizen. And it's nobody's damned business what your private life is like, anyway.

The *Playboy* philosophy here took the knife of individualism, sharpened it on the stone of antiquated legislated morality, and sliced into our repressed culture at the point of our most frustrating contradiction—namely, a Puritan conscience overlaid on an openly sensate consumer society. Hefner's seemingly prurient obsession with the body female was a gorgeous gauntlet thrown down to the body politic: let us in fact have separation of church and state, private morals and public legislation. He never tired of castigating outmoded laws designed to control everybody's conscience on the basis of a few religious leaders' version of what morality must be (blue laws, laws on homosexuality and premarital intercourse, laws on sexual relations within marriage itself, censorship laws). He consistently linked together the concepts of democracy, liberty, personal freedom, human reason, natural goodness of human desire, and he consistently contrasted all of these with the archaic ethic perpetrated on the new, vital, upbeat generation that would no longer tolerate such an erosion of natural rights in the name of God.

Thus Hefner has been considered by some a kind of prophet of the sexual revolution in our time. It might be more accurate to say that he was really the beneficiary of that revolution rather than its herald, its profit rather than its prophet. Earl Brill (*Sex Is Dead*) suggested, with more cleverness than insight, that Hefner was the

Billy Graham of the sensual set, a kind of sexual fundamentalist. Tom Wolfe (*The Pump House Gang*) tells us, with much greater insight, that Hefner's not about sex at all, but a new technocracy. After all, the mansion *is* a self-contained world of gadgets, revolving beds, "bat-cars," projection equipment, secret staircases (shades of Nancy Drew!)—even a $21,000 stereo set. Robinson called it "a sandbox for adults." Nelson Algren said it was an "automated tomb." In the sixties Hefner never left it for six months at a stretch. His great black bunny bird has made him more mobile for the seventies.

My point is that Hefner is an exact model of the fundamental contradiction in our technology-humanity interface. He was Mr. Super-Square who finally got introduced to Roundness. He was right in attacking laws that no longer fit our context of interpersonal relations. He was right in excoriating our self-righteousness and our "religious" otherworldliness. He was more correct than he knew when he stated flatly that our modern economic pressures and religious pretensions were absolutely antithetical. He was right when he assumed that the human body was nothing to be ashamed of, that sex is not some subhuman channel for original sin, or a primordial hangover from an anthropoid ancestry, and that life should be lived to the hilt without crippling inhibition concerning the passion of the life-force itself. Of course a young generation shouted hurray for Hugh—and to those who desisted on these points they quoted an ancient orison: "May the bird of paradise fly up your blue nose."

Eros Denied

Now the "Christian" community has typically provided the long flaring nostrils of that nose. The history of ecclesiastical sexual repression has been documented with stiletto precision by apologists from Derrick Baley (*Sexual Relation in Christian Thought*), William E. Phipps (*Was Jesus Married? The Distortion of Sexuality in Christian Tradition*), to Hefner's own *Playboy Philosophy*. Most of these are mere encyclopedias of festering libidos that in the end simply put us back in heaven in Cinerama. They nearly all conclude by telling us to be "responsible," which means—after the lugubrious rhetoric is drained off—a rewelding of the iron in our crotches.

There is one that does not. Written in 1964 by Wayland Young, a member of the British House of Lords, it is entitled *Eros Denied: Sex in Western Society*.[1] It is a spectacular narrative of sexual exclusion in the Christian psyche (words, images, actions, people).

The central teaching of Christianity, he tells us (more important than the incarnation and the atonement—which would make it fairly important!), is that God is One and that he loves man. It follows then that man will be "responsible," that is, respond to God's love by loving. Young quotes the first letter of John: "Herein is love; not that we loved God, but that He loved us." And further: "We love because He first loved us." And again: "Beloved if God so loved us, we ought also to love one another." (1 John 4). God, as all will agree, is greater than man, so naturally his love is not only prior, but greater. The greater (God's) must be visible through the lesser (man's) and the greater must always be visible, accessible to, and perfecting the lesser.

This sequence Young calls "the causal chain in the genesis of love," and he rightly sees the most appropriate analogy for it as the father's love for his children. The problem with this lovely model is that it is not suitable for men: it works only *before* the polarity of sex arises. Children are sexual, but only become one side of the polarity with the onset of puberty. The capacity for orgasm is the door that leads out of toyland. As men and women grow out of childhood and experience orgasm, their attention is radically distracted from the love of the Father. However intense their love for God may be at other times, at that moment they are absorbed with each other. Notions of "spiritual" love, "higher" or "greater" love, are swept aside by this passionate, primary love. Young, in passing, cites Kinsey's experimental verification of this phenomenon of intensity in erotic union. Kinsey—having graduated from wasp wings —fired pistols (!) in the same room without disturbing lovers at the brink. Jealous husbands, I would guess, report counter findings.

What we are treated to in eros is such an unusual concentration of energy that it actually *suspends reason* and temporarily relegates

God to oblivion. Both Augustine and Aquinas warned decisively against physical love for this reason, with Augustine having the best of it as the man who knew what he was warning against.

The "Christian" premise then is that the love of God is better than the love between a man and a woman because the latter interferes with the former. Paul gets a lot of blame in the sexual histories for his attitude toward women—in fact is usually fingered as the culprit in Christian misogyny. But if he were convinced that the Christ-Story had to be carried to *every* man in the Mediterranean world as quickly as possible, then he might well have been justified in thinking that eros would impede that mission. My point, later on, will be that a full-orbed reading of the Christ-Story would radically alter that proscription.

Nevertheless, as Young points out, *divine* love early in our history became an alternative to *sexual* love: chastity became one of the vows for the spiritually elite, virgins were holier than wives and indeed were brides of Christ, and some men of God who were particularly bothered by female distraction let it all hang out and castrated themselves. One quotation out of the arsenal of outraged libertines will sum up the decisive "Christian" attitude toward women, a choice description by Cardinal Hugues de St. Cher:

> Woman pollutes the body, drains the resources, kills the soul, uproots the strength, blinds the eye and embitters the voice.[2]

It occurs to me that one of the great humorists of history is lost to us—the man who named schools for clergy "seminaries." *Seedbed* for the spirit indeed! He undoubtedly spoke Sumerian.

It is with this background that we can see rebellion against authority manifesting itself as sexual permissiveness, for "God-language" in our culture usually functions as authority language. "Maturity," "responsible behavior," are secular versions of the same vocabulary. To engage in sexual activity, particularly for the young, is not exclusively an act of exquisite awareness of the body. It is also, and sometimes primarily, an act of defiance, a rape of the system. When Eldridge Cleaver confessed in *Soul On Ice* that he raped white women, we should have known instantly that he wasn't just another criminal psychopath (or practicing up for the "black" experience). He was locating a disease crippling Western man's full possibilities. James Baldwin had identified the disease long before Cleaver's genital pyrotechnics. In *The Fire Next Time* (which apparently will not only thaw the soul on ice but purge oppressive America) he takes us through his childhood in a Baptist Church, with the obvious purpose of showing us that the fulfillment of love is not possible on "Christian" soil.

> Yes, it does indeed mean something—something unspeakable—to be born in a white country, an Anglo-Teutonic, antisexual country, black. You very soon, without knowing it, give up all hope of communion.[3]

The white culture is a death culture, unwilling to embrace the life-force itself. Says Baldwin:

> White Americans . . . suspect that the force is sensual, and they are terrified of sensuality and do not any longer understand it.[4]

All these—the frustrating ambiguities, the prior claims of God's love, the denigration of women, the denial of eros and fear of sensuality, the unexamined demand for purity, not to mention the trivial address of our educational ghettos to the human condition—all these were the legacy of a man like Hefner. He was born the faithful son of devoted Methodists, who raised him with all the care of any good fundamental flustards. And he was candid enough to admit why he started *Playboy:* "I wanted to publish a magazine that would thumb its nose at all restrictions." It's not that far from thumbing noses to raping white women.

Hefner, however, refused to remain an insolent publisher. He became a theologian. In 1963 he wrote: "We're applying sixteenth-century religion to a twentieth-century world. A more sophisticated time requires a more sophisticated faith." Now the truth here is that we are mistaking sixteenth-century scientific models of thought for sixteenth-century religion and dragging that scientific model uncritically into the modern world. What we need is not a more sophisticated faith—one is not likely to find anything more cosmopolitan that Luther giving advice during the wedding ceremony on how to perform sexual intercourse. What we need is someone to show us how thought proceeds through the cultural patterns of any given era and that any judgment on the adequacy of a particular thought system must be made in the light of the *Weltanschauung* (every serious book has to have this word in it) out of which it came.

But the problem of definition of religion is secondary to Hefner's implicit assumption in this early misunderstanding; namely, that religious faith reflected the century, that it did not shape it. That since the modern mood and technological advance provide for the possibility of sexual license with minimal psychological effects, our religious faith ought to make room for this license. Thus Hefner does invoke the blessing of God as a rationale for his wonderful full-color foldouts: God made male and female and behold it was good.

But if God gets in the way of laissez-faire individualism then he is relegated to the sixteenth century. Which is in one sense to say, he is using God, manipulating the mystery of reality to serve his own exclusive purposes. This, I take it, is idolatry. It is idolatry when clergymen attempt to manipulate God by ritualism, prayers, and intellectual gamesmanship—perhaps even in written confessional celebrations. It is no less blasphemous when politicians or magazine editors do it, not even if the idolatry is less robed than the traditional cleric and much more fun for the fantasy life.

One remembers Norman Vincent Peale's famous story of how a man named Flynt made a million dollars by the time he was forty. Flynt, it seems, had always had this ambition, but somehow had failed until he heard Dr. Peale speak on having the faith of a grain of mustard seed. In the honorable tradition of American business elasticity, Flynt got himself a mustard seed, kept it in his pocket to remind him daily of that faith. Unfortunately this spiritual aid brought new problems: Flynt kept losing the tiny mustard seed. In the honorable tradition of American ingenuity, he had an idea. Why not encase the seed in plastic? Which he did. Then he had another —better—more enriching—idea. Perhaps there would be a market for mustard seed in plastic. There was: a million-dollar market— before Flynt was forty!

Following this stirring tale of faith—capitalism in our time—as told by Peale in a Methodist seminary chapel, the congregation sang Charles Wesley's triumphant "Oh, for a thousand tongues to sing my great Redeemer's praise." While the inspiration was fresh, a group of students wrote a new hymn more appropriate to our consumer society, and, during the dinner hour, sang it for Dr. Peale.

> Oh, for a thousand mustard seeds
> to spread among the race;
> The gospel of our Lord and King
> inside a plastic case.
>
> Flynt is the name that charms our fears,
> that bids our faith go far;
> When you're in need just take a seed
> from out the relish jar.

Peale's reaction was, of course, positive.

The Masculine Mystique

The *Playboy* myth continues to serve as a focus for the peculiar convolution of sexual liberation in this culture. Perhaps the clearest delineation of the problem occurred at the Cornell debate between Hefner and Harvey Cox.[5] The gist of the discussion was this. Adolescence and post-adolescence represents the crisis of identity for the male. What does the young man want to know above all things? How to be a man, a genuine *male,* with unmistakable virility.

It was to this question that *Playboy* addressed itself in what David Reisman called "the mass media peer group surrogate." *Playboy* was literally a "guidebook to identity," in Cox's phrase; "a contribution to the discovery of maleness," in Allen Moore's less pretentious terms. The upbeat generation male was to be cool, unruffled, detached—using all the latest consumer items with contemporaneous dexterity. He knew how to do everything with studied casualness and extraordinary facilty of adjustment. The Playboy's poise was impeccable. Styles change, jazz groups became passé, reading lists varied but the Playboy reacted to every shift with glacial adroitness, guided (according to Cox) into a male identity every bit as authoritative as Paul at Corinth or Lyndon at Atlantic City (Daley at Chicago?). *Playboy*'s pronouncements, he suggested, made "a papal encyclical sound irresolute."

In the Cornell debate Cox tellingly attacked the advisability of "casual sex," explicitly drawing the issue as "a question of promiscuity or intimacy." Now the cardinal symptom of the so-called Playboy male syndrome was supposed to be this: be unattached, resist involvement, existence is a romp, creation is fundamentally recreation.

This theme of unencumbered recreation is neither definitive of *Playboy* nor quite as lethal as Cox (and assorted mirror ministers) or even the husky-voiced witchery of Betty Friedan make it appear. It contains, in badly garbled voracious form, the germ of a truly redemptive life-style—a point to which we will return in the last chapter. Nevertheless, it laid *Playboy* open, and a hungry (!) host of critics poured in on that vulnerability. The theme was most dramatically demonstrated by the Playmate in the magazine and the Penmates in the Bunny Clubs. After all, what is the ultimate recreation? It's Peter Rabbit chasing little cotton tail. It's making Mary. It's one apocalyptic orgasm after another.

But the Playmate must understand the rule of this titillation game: after the ball is over the female partner recedes into the background with all that formless retinue of pleasurable objects. Under no circumstances must she get serious. All good American joke books tell us that a bachelor is a man who can get a woman in his arms without having her on his hands. The knight of pleasure—O modish chivalry—goes forth to war, proudly displaying his coat of arms: a tuxedoed rabbit on a field of black.

Given the history of sex in Christendom, we can all understand the male attraction to this approach, which should be labeled "The Woman as Nigger." Disraeli once said that all women should be married, but no man. But it is at least interesting—on reflection, startling—that a great many intelligent women (including many of the "chicks" in the campus radical movement) were taken in by the premise of women as playthings, objects to be used to gratify urges for the three *C*'s: companionship, conversation, and coitus—and on cue. (This translates into marriage as *Kirche, Küche,* and *Kinder.*) Mimi Drennan, onetime Mother Superior of the Bunny Hutch in Detroit, expressed it decisively. Explaining Operation Bunny she said: "She is supposed to decorate the room." This is the kind of statement that cosmically infuriates the Women's Liberation Front and sends them boiling into battle. Detractors of the movement insist they have no fronts with which to decorate.

Despite Hefner's disclaimers at all recent Women's Lib vs. Male Chauvinist debates, this still seems to be the real concept of woman's role in *Playboy*. She decorates—the magazine, the living room, the swimming pool, the bedroom. Cox insisted that like any good accessory she was disposable or replaceable or should just lie there until needed again. I should think that Hefner might now reply that in the considerable female revolution under way the problem of disposability and "plaything" works both ways: that it is quite possible for a woman to use a man as a prestigious instrument, as a stud, or as a stepping-stone. Superwoman might smile to the girls back at the sorority house: "Wow! Did my little teeth-lined vagina chew him to pieces!" Whichever way it worked, Playboy or Playgirl, given any growth toward true humanness, male or female, we would have to put it down as adolescent. Immanuel Kant (was Ayn Rand *serious?*) informed us over two hundred years ago that we must never use a person as a means only.

There was another use for this body object specified by Cox, and here Hefner again mirrored the corporate sickness of America, so advertised by Charles Reich's love affair with Berkeley. The Plaything was the new icon supporting the value system of a crass materialism, symbolizing our consumer society just as the Virgin Mary symbolized the ideals of medieval society. Only the Plaything was not the Virgin. She was by definition *not* the Virgin. She was in fact the Anti-Virgin, the inverted Madonna who represented an exact reversal of a value complex (of poverty, humility, and sacrifice) which nourished Western civilization from the time of the first Christmas. Cox put it this way:

> In startling contrast, particularly to the portrait of Mary in Luke 1: 46–50, the girl has nothing to do with filling the hungry with good things, hawking instead an endless proliferation of trivia on TV spot commercials.[6]

What is clear now from this distance is that Cox's put-down was not only misplaced, but that it failed to point to the appropriateness, to the *health,* of Hefner's sexual protest. A faithful son, coming alive, *should* publish a theological journal for frustrated Methodists (and Baptists, to get Cox in), and the form of that protest would naturally be *consumption,* since that is precisely where American affluence is centered. We really *don't* need a virginal Miss America!

Sex in an entrepreneurial society must turn into "unencumbered recreation" as an oblique protest to the system. If it fails to drive the society toward more wholeness in human life, it stays in the system. It stays in the system as protest only as a sport, a game to be won or lost, a battle of the sexes.

One of the most imaginative of these protest movements formed at Pacific and used with delicious irony this misunderstanding of sex as competitive sport. Big-time, ceremonious athletics in colleges everywhere are in trouble financially and philosophically, and we were no exception. One deadly, playful, faculty radical (John Morearty) decided to protest the *Support Pacific Football* (S.P.F.) program (inspired by Amos Alonzo Stagg, and producing, in order, Eddie LeBaron, Dick Bass, a stadium seating 34,000—for a student body of 1,000 when it was built—and a fabulous annual deficit) with a counter-culture group he called S.P.S. These letters translated as Support Pacific Screwing. He gathered a goodly throng of students for a rally speech, the full text of which I will not quote. The general level of the speech ran to bonfire pitches like these: "We'll still use the stadium," . . . "All the equipment you need you already have," and "think of the homecoming parade!" The bright orange bumper stickers Morearty printed up put the town alumni into orbit, and prompted the head football coach to announce publicly: "Anybody who doesn't support college football is a Communist." Morearty might have replied rather glumly that the Reds are more associated with baseball, but he was rushed off to our India campus. I contented myself with rereading Norman Mailer's *Why Are We in Vietnam?*

Yes, the time is soon coming, thinks Rusty, when fornication will be professional athletics, and everybody will watch the national eliminations on TV. Will boys like D.J. and Tex be in the finals with a couple of Playboy bunnies or black-ass honeys? [7]

When the capacity for orgasm diverts our attention from powers celestial in a competitive culture, its *natural* perversions are titillation, the Cheshire leer, line drawing, erotic gladiatorial contests, and genital *hubris*. A "jock" is the exact vernacular for one who withdraws into masturbation, instead of marching on to the battleground of manhood. This is the beginning of pigdom, a pecking order of protest that defies authority from above by sexually assaulting everything in the environment. Since sex is "beneath" the love of God, it is therefore psychologically degrading, and neutralizes the power of that which it attacks. The forms of this twisted use of sensuality all have the smell of violence on them, and their proper genre is consumption. The military establishment escalating conflict, the corporate state maintaining a hegemony over the individual, the brutalizing of minorities, the rape of the land, the transformation of student into nigger, the lobotomization of women, the acceleration of spectator sports: all these are symptoms of our national disease, of which the deflowered virgin is the great symbol. She is the tarnished miracle, the arrogance of innocence put in its place.

The Women's Liberation Movement has attacked this with the kind of vengeance that may bring off the most fundamental revolution in our culture. One of the underground pieces now circulating in the movement is called "The Peculiar Alienation of High School Women." After sketching out the problem of sex as a pastime in an acquisitive culture (high-school boys in their insolent insecurity getting trained for manhood by watching their fathers beating up their mothers, going to bars, observing older brothers getting flashy cars, taking out a new girl every night and to the pulsing of Hendrix on the stereo "balling" hell out of her), the essay identifies *the* adolescent symbol of the problem.

A cheerleader is a key figure in high school women's oppression. She's the Uncle Tom. All at once, she is a sex symbol, a virginity symbol, and the symbol of the all-American good girl.

It is a painful, pathetic sight, this girl caught in the crush of what a girl has to become in order to be consumed.

To watch a sister executing her cheer before an audience is to witness the symbolic drama of a high school woman's struggle for survival and acceptance. Her face is frozen into a false submissive grin or a look of fierce concentration as she whirls and gyrates—and inherent in that face are traces of desperation and helplessness at being on display for her body. Out in the audience, seated behind the drooling wolves, are her sisters—echoing that same cry as they sit silently hating the sister on the stage, and hating themselves.

Hefner's Plaything is the real Miss America the cherub-faced song girl: plastically sexual, conferring her charismatic charm on all our pseudo-sensuality—neckties, watch charms, cigars, sweaters, draped on the back of a motorcycle, lips caressing sparkling Champale, languidly inviting on a downy pillow, shaving lotion balanced on her pert head, staring worshipfully at a bowl full of tobacco. The Atlantic City pageant certainly ought to add to their death culture panel the editor of *Playboy,* who knows what beauty is and does, who knows that women are measurements—finely calibrated arrangements of pleasurable utility sanctifying our unredeemed capitalism with promise of amoral tumescence. There she unfolds: your ideal.

This is not another put-down of *Playboy.* There is something weirdly emancipating about all this non-sense, some beginning of wisdom obscured demonically by the strident male chauvinistic commercialism, but also suggesting, in a professionally square way, that the world could be round. In the late fifties and early sixties, *Playboy* was a "radical" publication. But while it began a process of emancipation, it could only consume, and by failing to deepen its protest continues into the seventies as a "conservative" institution. The prophet has become the enemy. Yet he is not without honor.

No More Masterpieces

So Baldwin called us an "anti-sexual country" (still longing no doubt for "another country"). And Harvey Cox tagged *Playboy*'s pumpkin-breasted voyeurism with that same line. My opinion is that they are both wrong. What appears as fear of sensuality to Baldwin and anti-sexuality to Cox is really semi-sexuality—a beginning, an awakening, that hardens into racism on the one hand and shimmers off into permissive cultism on the other. When the sexual genesis of racism is revealed, we can understand why freedom must be expressed in love and unfreedom in the repression of the body.

Now one implacable enemy of freedom is competition, which expresses itself in the failure of intimacy between man and woman. No one can be intimate while trying to win, and no one can be free while running a race. One is always glancing over one's shoulder to see how close the opposition is. Freedom in fascism means freedom only to maintain position, only to assume power, and power is useless (noncompetitive) unless it is in fact power over something. This, says Mailer, is "why we are in Vietnam": our military posture is our national phallus stuck in the soft underbelly of Indochina, a last chance to shine up our "fast-rusting barbs." The underground (street-corner) press featured a cartoon depicting President Nixon unzipping Uncle Sam's fly—and out pops a ballistic missile!

Antonin Artaud had another name for this "semi-sexuality." He called it a "petty sensuality," and argued that contemporary theater should no longer produce "masterpieces," but instead a "theater of cruelty" to teach us that we are not yet free.

> I propose to return through the theater to an idea of the physical knowledge of images and the means of inducing trances, as in Chinese medicine which knows, over the entire extent of the human anatomy, at what points to puncture in order to regulate the subtlest functions.
>
> Those who have forgotten the communicative power and magical mimesis of a gesture, the theater can reinstruct, because a gesture carries its energy with it, and there are still human beings in the theater to manifest the force of the gesture made.
>
> To create art is to deprive a gesture of its reverberation in the organism, whereas this reverberation, if the gesture is made in the conditions and with the force required, incites the organism and, through it, the entire individuality, to take attitudes in harmony with the gesture.
>
> The theater is the only place in the world, the last general means we still possess of directly affecting the organism and, in periods of neurosis and petty sensuality like the one in which we are immersed, of attacking this sensuality by physical means it cannot withstand.[8]

The function of theater, then, is to make contact with the audience as a total organism, as completely sensuous beings—to use our pettiness as a wedge into wholeness, so that we can at last understand cruelty as the inverse of titillation. It is not really so vicious to be charmed back into our full bodies.

> If music affects snakes, it is not on account of the spiritual notions it offers them, but because snakes are long and coil their length upon the earth, because their bodies touch the earth at almost every point; and because the musical vibrations which are communicated to the earth affect them like a very subtle, very long massage; and I propose to treat the spectators like the snakecharmer's subjects and conduct them *by means of their organisms* to an apprehension of the subtlest notions.[9]

This would mean the end of theater as performance, as separation between audience and spectators. Indeed, Susan Sontag (*Against Interpretation*) demonstrates brilliantly that Peter Weiss' play, *The Persecution and Assassination of Jean Paul Marat as Performed by the Inmates of the Asylum at Charenton under the Direction of the Marquis de Sade,* incarnates this understanding of theater. The play within that play ends with the inmates (the "cast" of Sade's play) physically attacking the audience (M. Coulmier, the director of the asylum, and his family). This riot is ended by the entry of the stage manager (in modern shirt, sweater, and gym shoes) who blows a whistle signaling finis. As the "real" audience applauds, the "actors" mock that applause with slow and ominous handclap that drowns out the "free" response. (I never knew in *Curious* when we were in the "film" and when we were in the "explanation of the filming.")

The demand by Jerry Farber in *The Student as Nigger* that the grading system be changed to *credit–no credit* was simply another pressure to dethrone the hierarchy of competitive values. Grades (masterpieces) niggerize the student, performances niggerize the actors, sports niggerize the athletes, armies niggerize the soldiers. As Kurt Vonnegut, Jr.'s bemused tonic slides us through *Slaughter House Five:* "And so it goes." The fire bombing of Dresden *was* great theater. And so it goes.

The Playboys of the Western World must continue their protest within the consumer system, for it is precisely that system which has made them possible, while at the same time making their rebellion necessary. They will continue to color within the lines, and do all things decently and in order. Hefner's entrepreneurial sexual revolution is simon-pure legally. The Chicago Bunny Club is constructed with the most exact attention to the building code.

To put the matter as paradoxically as possible, Hugh Hefner does not belong in bed with his playmates. His real bedfellow is William F. Buckley, Jr. They both present themselves impeccably before the throne of corporate individualism, with total, law-abiding calm. The one achieved respectability; the other had it thrust upon him. Hefner's Methodism and Buckley's Catholicism both still serve as screens upon which they project their philosophies of liberation. When Buckley's sister physically attacked a Women's Lib spokesman—spokeswoman—at a Catholic University forum, for insulting the Virgin Mary, I hope Hefner was applauding vigorously—not in mockingly slow, ominous claps. His very existence as an American Culture Myth depends on keeping Our Lady unsullied. Nonvirginity as a consumer icon makes no sense without veneration of the Virgin. Hail Mary, full of cash!

The situation which we have been diagnosing is more than a disease. It is really *insanity*—this schizophrenic separation between the body and the spirit, pleasure and reason, sensibility and idea, reality and symbol. Such freedom as we do possess has to be applied somewhere to heal this split. Neurotics, it is said, build castles in the air, schizophrenics live in them, and psychiatrists collect the rent off of them. One might say that Christendom built the repressive castle, Middle America bought it, and Hefner lives comfortably off the interest it creates.

Artaud's suggestion of a "theater of cruelty" and a "poetry of festivals" had merit as an alternative to sexual consumer protest within the system, and the remarkable incarnation in *Marat/Sade* embodies that suggestion. The play is a play within a play, and when the audience is constantly lured into being part of the play and finally accosted, it becomes a theatrical hall of mirrors, endlessly reflecting both the players and ourselves, rather as if there were no play at all, but only reality. The "setting" of the "play" is a madhouse where the Marquis de Sade is allowed to present to the inmates a dramatic re-creation of the French Revolution. His antagonist is Jean Paul Marat, who is finally assassinated by Charlotte Corday as he stares unblinkingly from his bathtub coffin and reels off in robot fashion stunningly revolutionary ideas about man's ability to change history. Sade counters with the argument that "the world is made of bodies," and all revolution therefore is quite hopeless since man's nature is fixed (conditioned by his environment). In one exceptionally powerful scene, Sade agonizes out these ideas while Charlotte whips him with her hair. The intent, Artaud-like, is not to distract the audience, but to suggest that ideas themselves are *sensory*. By shifting our focus off the characters onto the *intensity* of the characters, we are ushered into an emotional experience of our own—an erotic, flagellation experience. As Susan Sontag put it: The use of language is *incantation* and acting becomes *ritual*.

When the entire cast bursts into a paroxysm of song and simulates all varieties of sexual intercourse as they sing, the point is irresistible:

> And what's the point of a revolution
> without general
> copulation copulation copulation*

Madhouse? Insanity? This is a *play?* No cool, detached characters here. Sontag comments:

> Insanity becomes the privileged, most authentic metaphor for passion; or, what's the same thing in this case, the logical terminus of any strong emotion. Both dream (as in the "Marat's Nightmare" sequence) and dream-like states must end in violence. Being "calm" amounts to a failure to understand one's real situation.[11]

At some point in this insane society, sexual protest just explodes out of its consumer model. Freedom and physical love are too tightly bound up with one another to do otherwise. No more masterpieces, no decorum, no rules and boundaries, no submission to the judges of art or the commercial market. No more "immoral" behavior masquerading behind the superstructure of orthodoxy.

If Apollo "comes," can Dionysus be far behind?

* From *The Persecution and Assassination of Jean Paul Marat as Performed by the Inmates of the Asylum at Charenton under the Direction of the Marquis de Sade* by Peter Weiss. Copyright © 1965 by John Calder Ltd. English version by Geoffrey Skelton, verse adaptation by Adrian Mitchell. Permission granted by Atheneum Publishers.

5

Receiving:
A Rebirth of Wonder

Once upon a time, a very ordinary young man, the son of a well-to-do merchant, got a sudden flash of insight. Though friends were shocked and relatives dismayed, he junked his expensive wardrobe and walked out of his father's opulent home to spend the rest of his life singing and telling people about God and love. Lots of people still think Saint Francis was some kind of nut. He wanted everybody to stop trying to get rich and to live in joyous poverty. He refused to make any provision for the next day, since he thought that would cast doubts on God's beneficence. He looked with contempt on book learning and put his trust in feelings. He annoyed the religiously orthodox by preaching to the birds, composing canticles to the sun and pandering a whimsical kind of pantheism. Yet he was eventually made a saint.

Eight hundred years later, thousands of American young people stopped cutting their hair, discarded Ivy League suits and walked out of their parents' suburban palaces to prance barefoot through the streets, strum guitars and tell us all to make love and not war. Fourteen-year-olds who used to attend meetings of Methodist youth groups began to paint their faces chrome yellow, writhe to the rhythm of Indian sitars and wear buttons that tell the world I LOVE EVERYBODY.

HARVEY COX
"God and the Hippies"
Playboy Magazine, XV, January, 1968

While slipping into his clothes, adjusting the drum round his neck, stowing his drumsticks under his suspenders, Oskar carried on negotiations with his two gods Dionysus and Apollo. The god of unreflecting drunkenness advised me to take no reading matter at all, or if I absolutely insisted on reading matter, then a little stack of Rasputin would do; Apollo, on the other hand, in his shrewd, sensible way, tried to talk me out of this trip to France altogether, but when he saw that Oskar's mind was made up, insisted on the proper baggage; very well, I would have to take the highly respectable yawn that Goethe had yawned so long ago, but for spite, and also because I knew that *The Elective Affinities* could never solve all my sexual problems, I also took Rasputin and his naked women, naked but for their black stockings. If Apollo strove for harmony and Dionysus for drunkenness and chaos, Oskar was a little demigod whose business it was to harmonize chaos and intoxicate reason.

GÜNTER GRASS
The Tin Drum

What the great world needs, of course, is a little more Eros and less strife; but the intellectual world needs it just as much.

NORMAN O. BROWN
Life Against Death

The Redemption of the Robot

Years ago floating up on the suds of the old-time radio serials was one called "Mr. Keen, Tracer of Lost Persons." His job, as I recall, was to seek out people who had simply vanished. When Johnson was escalating the war in Vietnam, accompanied by knowing smiles from Arizona, one of the blackest buttons around read: "Where is Oswald now that we need him?" With the events in our nation producing what Roszak termed the "counter-culture"—the disaffected middle-class American youth—and prompting Kenneth Keniston to identify that "youth" (eighteen to twenty-five) as a brand-new "stage" in the American maturation process, I thought the time was ripe for a new button: "Where is Mr. Keen, now that we need him?"

The new Mr. Keen was a professor of theology at Louisville Presbyterian (*selah*) Seminary, that's where. In 1969 in *Cross*

Currents he surfaced with an article entitled "Manifesto for a Dionysian Theology," which he later expanded into a scholarly book making an *Apology for Wonder* and a biographical celebration addressed *To a Dancing God*. The portable Keen is embedded in the manifesto and still worth carrying around, for it hinted at a way to move beyond the death of God without either worshipping acquisitive secularism or dusting off the *deus ex machina* (shrouded so thoroughly by the nineteenth century and resurrected subsequent to the assassination of John F. Kennedy). *Time* naturally, in high camp style, heralded Sam Keen as a member of a new school of "God is Alive" theologians, a group including Keen and Harvey Cox (who now was moving beyond his *Secular City* prudery and beginning to enjoy some unencumbered recreation himself, and was suggesting in print that "Christ the Harlequin" did the same).

Keen begins by quoting Nietzsche: "I could only believe in a god who could dance." He continues by resummarizing for us the distinction between Apollo and Dionysus—the history of that distinction running from Norman O. Brown to Herbert Marcuse, through Günter Grass and Nikos Kazantzakis to Nietzsche, then all the way back to Aeschylus and *The House of Atreus*. Apollo is the god of sanity, discipline, order. He brings us light, reason, and balance. An Apollonian culture specializes in setting boundaries and learning rules. Whatever impulses run counter to this order must be repressed. The Apollonian way, he reminds us, had come to dominate Western culture.

Furthermore, our culture organizes *psychic* space in the same way that it orders *physical* space. To become a "mature" person in this society means to *internalize* that order in such a way that external force need no longer press us into place. Coercion is replaced by "responsibility."

Dionysus is the god of license, energy, chaos. He brings us ecstasy, causes us to stand outside ourselves (*ex stasis*), literally makes us beside ourselves. He breaks through the boundaries and explodes psychic space. He cannot be controlled. Dionysus in our culture is always *just under* the surface of order and wherever freedom is proscribed by tyranny, he breaks loose and dethrones the tyrant. Decorum is replaced by orgy.

Keen, in good Apollonian fashion, charts the distinction I have drawn:

The Apollonian Way	*The Dionysian Way*
Man - the - maker, fabricator, molder and manipulator of environment.	Man - the - dancer responding to the givenness of life in its multiplicity.
Domination of the ego, emphasis upon erecting boundaries, giving form, intellectual and material possession. The will and the intellect are central.	Domination of the id. Emphasis upon destroying boundaries, exploration of diversity, chaos, vitality. Feeling and sensation are central.
Value is created by action, Authentic life is aggressive, "masculine," active.	Value is discovered, it is given as we encounter the world in wonder. Authentic life involves passivity, accepting, responding.[1]

The translation of this schemata into a Dionysian theology is compelling: we are to allow ourselves to become open to insecurity, to creaturehood, to animality. We must return to the most primitive meaning of the Scripture that the *earth* is the Lord's. *This means no longer possessing, but being possessed.*

This is a delicate point. How can we reconcile this approach with our whole first emphasis on intentionality? If we must seize our own lives, are we not back in some fundamental contradiction to *allow* ourselves to be seized?

On the contrary, I think we are in direct line with decisional Christianity. The Jesus-Christ-Event releases us for the first time to really see the world as a given. Before that event I was forever attempting to control my world as insulation from my anxiety that I may cease to be. *Then* my possession is a sickness, for by ordering the earth I say *no* to my own sure dissolution. The early Christian warning against loving the things of this world meant, I take it, exactly that.

The Jesus-Christ-Event delivers us into radical freedom, which means that I am free to love the things of earth *without* possessing them. They in fact possess me, enrapture me, complete me into a living part of them. *I choose to be possessed.*

Now in case we don't recognize it right off, this is what I read as the Christian doctrine of grace. "Grace" means unmerited favor, and implies to many an outdated and particularly commercial way of allowing "God" back on his old heteronomous throne, damning some and saving others, as he wills.

I prefer the *natural* meaning of "grace": the grace of an athlete responding to stress with a power born out of his own body but charming his arena of stress on its own ground. We use the resistance of the air to leap, the buoyancy of the water to glide, the weight of an object to swing. The free human being is graceful; he is possessing life as a gift.

> I sought the Lord, and afterward I knew
> He moved my soul to seek Him, seeking me.
> It was not I who found, Oh Saviour true.
> No, I was found by Thee.

This is not piety. It is Dionysian reality: the very oldest time religion!

It is obvious then that we do not abandon Apollo, for unlimited freedom is as much an illness as total tyranny is a sickness. Our problem is summed up in one of the great fiction characters of our time: Oskar the dwarf in Grass's *The Tin Drum*. Oskar refuses to grow (sound familiar?), and covers his dwarfed potential by drumming. His drum is also his childish brain, and with his two drumsticks he tattoos thoughts so great they are capable of disrupting even the most strident of charismatic dictators—his drumming shatters a Nazi rally. Then one day, early in adolescence he discovers a third drumstick, a marvelously cute and versatile little drumstick even more useful than his tongue or his fingers searching for "raspberries" on a woman's belly (and his "Maria was rich in raspberries").

> . . . my tongue gave up and I grew an eleventh finger, for my ten fingers proved inadequate for the purpose. And so Oskar acquired a third drumstick—he was old enough for that. And instead of drumming on tin, I drummed on moss.[2]

Oskar is still mystified by his delightful discovery. Does he possess it, or does it possess him?

Did the little gentleman down there have a mind and a will of his own? Who was doing all this: Oskar, he, or I? [3]

When he is twenty-one, the answer is clear. Oskar confesses to himself that he had killed his own father quite deliberately because "he was sick of dragging a father around with him all his life." He had spent more than seventeen years standing behind those hundred or so toy drums, so carefully lacquered red and white. Now standing before the freshly dug grave of his father he becomes a man.

> At this point he unslung the drum from his neck, no longer saying "Should I or shouldn't I?" but instead: "It must be," and threw the drum where the sand was deep enough to muffle the sound. I tossed in the sticks too . . . The sand piled up on my drum, the sand mounted and grew—and I too began to grow . . . .[4]

His friend Leo, astounded and seized, gyrates, dances into a fatal paroxysm, shouting all the while: "He's growing, he's growing . . ."

He didn't grow very much—few of us do—but this new awareness of his body was the beginning of his "intoxication of reason," and this new awareness of his intention was the beginning of his "harmonizing of chaos."

The mosaic form of my own confessional structures a witness that the most redemptive place to look for this intoxicating harmony is in the arts.

The aesthetic dimension of human life is in some sense conceptual, but this is not its main function. Nor is it simply animal sensuality—and I do not intend anything snide about our brothers in the bush. It is a third force: neither primarily intellectual nor appetitive. It is not even really a force perhaps—more a way, an opening, an unfolding. Herbert Read (the British artist who wrote the introduction to Camus' *The Fall*) sees it as "the redemption of the robot" since it allows the mask of individualism to merge into the real face behind it: allows, if you will, Apollo to merge with Dionysus, freedom materializing into love.

Art, as I perceive it, is fundamentally Christian because it is *sensuous*. That is, it gives us cognition through being affected by given objects. The aesthetic perception gives us pleasure through contact with form. The purpose of form is beside the point. It simply gives out its pleasure on contact and therefore becomes subjective to whomever it is contacting. The beauty of the moment of contact (perception) resides both in the form and in the person. Or rather, beauty comes into being as person and form meet. Words, for example, are not only designed to communicate ideas. They are, in themselves, ideas—forms of beauty that, appropriately received, may result in communion between speaker and spoken with. To put it biblically: the Word may become flesh. It does so *only* when it is received—*beheld,* in liturgical language—as of the glory of the Father.

Here then is the key point: *the nature of sensuousness is receptivity.*[5] To be is to be receptive, to be open, to give up our childish drumming and receive our own bodies. Just as resisting and consuming are the first stages of the humanizing drama, so emptying and receiving are the second. They correspond quite exactly to the traditional "plan of salvation" translated into the jargon of theologians as *conviction of sin* and *justification by grace through faith alone.* It is just here that most "culture Christians" have allowed themselves to be prostituted by the death culture (competitiveness), when in fact imaginal Christianity, the intentional Word-Event, is nothing other than the life culture (openness).

The Fine Art of Being Raped

This third "force" needs further definition in relation to receptivity, and particularly as it relates to the historic Christian community. I have said that grace is art: the creation of beauty in the meeting of subject and object. We are on the verge of an axial point, our understanding of which will move us from "petty sensuality" as protest into something manifestly Christian: our total embrace of the pleasures of earth, a sensuous Christianity. What is needed for this understanding is a closer look at the meaning of art.

"Art does not reproduce the visible; rather it makes visible," wrote Paul Klee, apparently an artist with no reluctance to reflect on his work as an artist. He was a painter, he said. "Color has me." "Color and I are one." And the meaning of his commitment to color was, in his words, "transposing things into the transcendent." Ben Shahn also confessed to being a painter, but talked less freely about why. In a series of lectures entitled *The Shape of Content* he expressed this severe reticence:

> I have come to Harvard with some very serious doubts as to whether I ought to be here at all.
> I am a painter; I am not a lecturer about art nor a scholar of art. It is my chosen role to paint pictures, not to talk about them.
> What can any artist bring to the general knowledge or the theoretical view of art that has not already been fully expounded? What can he say in words that he could not far more skillfully present in pictorial form? Is not the painting rather than the printed page his testament? Will he not only expend his energies without in any way increasing the general enlightenment? And then, what can an audience gain from listening to an artist that it could not apprehend far more readily simply by looking at his pictures? [6]

Both Klee's insights and Shahn's admonitions were awakened in me by an artist of luminous black eros, a certain Larry Walker. Preparing to attend a lecture on the nature of art, I was reading David Harned's *Theology and the Arts,* carrying it about like a flag of conquest over those mysterious odysseys of the flesh and spirit. Only a few yards from a pretentious center for cultural studies, Professor Walker unnerved my linear confidence in Harned's exposition.

"I'm learning about art," I said cheerfully. With gentle disdain, Mr. Walker replied, "In a book?"

Now Mr. Walker knew that the library is fat with excellent reading of the theory of aesthetics, and bloated with definitions and criticisms delineating artistic excellence. He might have directed me to Philip Beam's one-thousand-page *tour de force* on *The Language of Art* where Beam accepts Ducasse's definition of art as "the controlled objectification of feeling." He might have quoted Goethe's famous epigram: "Art is art because it is not nature." Or he could have even sent me to an old issue of the *Raymond Review* in which sculptor Mowry Baden suggested that art is the artifact of quarreling perceptual mechanisms, that man himself is art as he acts to test his own senses.

But he did not. He rebuked me. Finally the only way to learn about art is not to "learn about" it at all but to *look,* to *feel,* to *hear*—and to *read,* but only as participant. These sensory, "spiritual" evocations of the self in art are the real four-letter words that climax in love and life. The ultimate obscenity is to cut ourselves off from experiencing the wonder and directions of clustering energy.

Art has always, therefore, been the most incorrigible antagonist of censorship. It was a dangerously silly sign, for example, when our Supreme Court ruled that it was criminal to create an American flag shaped like a male sex organ, on par I should think with Hitler's banning of Mickey Mouse. The very first freedom to be suppressed in dictatorship is artistic expression, particularly the communicative arts. The control, the discipline in art, is not over the feeling, but over the form's appropriateness to the feeling. And this, I take it, is no proper subject for legislation.

Ralph Stephenson and J. R. Debrix rest a whole theory of film on the distinction between form and feeling. In *The Cinema as Art* they divide artistic activity into three stages:

1) The artist's experience or intuition,
2) Expression of this intuition in an artistic medium, and
3) Enjoyment by, and ideally the kindling of similar experiences in, an audience.[7]

In film all three elements tend to coalesce, though one and two are more obvious here than three. Intuition merges into execution in such a way that the spectator, unless he is especially perceptive, is not aware that some assumption, some directorial experience or understanding, is being made visible. Some transcendence is being transposed by technique. *Bullitt,* for example, won an Academy award for film editing, but how many of us noticed that superb montage when we saw the picture? The cutting, at the direction of Peter Yates, was absolutely flat, with no fade-ins or fade-outs, iris out and ins, dissolve or swipes—with the exception of one fade at the very end. Why? Yates called it "a new speed of perception," and Arthur Knight commented in *Saturday Review* that *Bullitt* was "completely typical of the 'now' look in American movies—swift-moving, constantly shifting surface that suggests rather than reveals depths." [8]

In Jules Dassin's *He Who Must Die* the film ends with the pilgrim peasants girding for final combat with the priest-dominated villages. Dassin is supposedly filming a novel, Kazantzakis' *The Greek Passion,* but in the novel the ending is quite different. There the peasants, remembering the ungracious villagers and clergy who refused to give sanctuary to the poor, trudge wearily away with all their belongings, shaking the dust off their feet. Why this difference between the novel and the picture? Dassin, of course, is a Marxist, who wants to show the poor in final apocalyptic battle against the rich, the established, the religious. Only when he has his hero address the poor can that hero speak without stuttering.

Stephenson and Debrix conclude their introductory chapter with this summary of film discipline as art:

> The film world possesses an anthropomorphic quality common to all arts which helps to create a deliberate emotional and mental effect in the spectator simply because, in the making, the film has been charged with this quality by the artist. Scenes which exist in nature are emotionally and dramatically "neutral," in the sense that they do not seek to move or influence us at the bidding of any exterior will. If an aurora borealis fills us with wonder, or a storm makes us afraid, the emotion comes from within ourselves; nobody has staged them with the express purpose of producing a reaction from an audience. But the images of a film are impregnated with the essence of the film-maker's own feeling and imaginings, and they become mental images as much as physical. They are designed not only to affect the senses but also to seize the imagination, and they even have a dynamic power of arousing the spectator's emotions by subtly following the changing movements of his own inner thought. The natural scene is *there*. It stays detached. It can be enjoyed, but remains aloof, indifferent. But the film as a work of art is deliberately made to attack us, to force its way into our feeling and our beliefs.[9]

So the artist focuses his insight, intrudes his meaning into our perception. I would assume that the greater the work the more devastating the intrusion, and because of this assumption I would like to suggest a way to fulfill Mr. Walker's admonition.

I have referred earlier to the special symposium at Albion College we called VIM. Each year we featured a motion picture for discussion, usually introducing it with all sorts of reviews and internal interpretations. The year Mathews visited us I asked him to introduce Orson Welles' *The Trial* (Kafka Agonistes). He did—and never mentioned the film at all.

> There is a story of a beautiful Indian woman. She was married to a blacksmith, big, fat, greasy and smelly. They had been married for a good many years when they decided to take a trip: so they went out and got in a broken-down old wagon and set out across the wasteland. When it got dark they stopped at a dirty, old, broken inn. It got very late and the woman decided to get up and sneak out. She crept along in the shadows so that nobody could see her and made for the edge of town. In those days there was a huge wall built around the edge of the town to shut out the chaos—strangers and animals. She got out to the wall, and, looking around to make sure no one was watching, she climbed up on the wall. As she looked out into the abyss, she was raped by the mystery. She was raped by the future. She was raped by sheer possibility, by incomprehensible intentionality. She was raped by globality. She fell back on the wall. Soon she got up and crept back, being careful that no one could see her, and mystery of mysteries, crawled in bed with her dirty, smelly, greasy blacksmith husband.

Not many in the audience recognized this as "The Adulterous Woman," by Albert Camus.

Like the unfaithful woman in Mathews' version of Camus' story, that is how to watch a motion picture, to experience theater, be present to a painting, a novel, some poetic vision. Let it rape you, intrude into your depths. Let it awaken the mystery of humanness in you. Let it strip you, make you, create life in you.

Now this is a powerful image, but I would include some more gentle, less vicious models of address to art. Often art is impotent when called on to perform brazenly, just as some men are. Often art needs to be loved before it reveals itself to us. This, I think, is the function of the great teacher of art appreciation. He brings us patience as spectators, shows us that discipline lies not only with the artist, but with the art lover, show us that our gelatinous bafflement at *Last Year at Marienbad,* our bemused irritation at Ussachevsky's electronic sound effects and John Cage's prepared piano, our boredom with Bach's mathematical mechanics, our snide moralism in the face of sensuous, numinous dance such as Ann Halprin's *Ceremony of Us,* our superficial titillation at Henry Miller's uncompromising honesty—that day after tomorrow these same reactions may be transformed, that our teacher has truly helped us to see, to hear, to touch, to be. It was for these reasons that Ingmar Bergman called himself a magician:

> When I show a film I am guilty of deceit . . . I take advantage of a certain human weakness . . . thus I am an impostor, or in the case where the audience is willing to be taken in, a conjurer. . . .[10]

The question might be put this way: what constitutes a "religious" dramatic art form? Asked this directly, we have then to distinguish between religious drama and drama which is religious.

Religious drama is drama whose content is specifically religious in an ecclesiastical or biblical way. Thus *J.B.* is religious drama and *The King of Kings* (tell it not in Gath) is religious cinema. In the glorious yesterdays De Mille (De Miracle?) made such "religious cinema" as *The Sign of the Cross* (too bad the cat at Claudette Colbert's milk bath wasn't really thirsty) and *The Ten Commandments* (in which, as Cox commented, De Mille succeeded in making Moses into a combination of Superman and Daniel Boone). The college crowd should have added at least one more non-negotiable demand to their list: that *no more* "religious" movies be made by Hollywood. And where one is shown the students ought to march around the theater seven times hoping the walls will fall down flat.

On the other hand, drama which is religious is drama whose content evokes *ontological* response from its participants; that is, when the spectator not only becomes part of the art experience through empathy, but also understands some new dimension about himself as a human being. It is theater which is revelatory, provides what Tillich called "ecstatic intuition," when the play or picture is not just communication (I got it), but communion (It got me).

In a profound sense it is illustrative of the poverty and prostitution of "religion" in our culture which allows us to separate religion and theater. Vincent de Gregoris, in an article entitled "Possibilities of Theater," reviewed the history of the drama as "the history of man seeking to make sense of human existence." [11] This history began around the sacrificial altar—so that worship, drama and theater have a common origin.

At first by the rhythms and cadences of the dance, man sought new sources of power in his struggle for survival and meaning. Early man's understanding of life was bodied forth in initiation ceremonies and ritual. In these dramatic forms he transmitted his myths, his images, his models of the world secret. The combination of mask and movement was the genesis of both religious expression and theater.

Greek drama, as we know, grew out of sacred dance and choral hymns sung to Dionysus around his altar. Worshippers of Dionysus, the god of animals, believed that in eating the raw flesh of animals and drinking new wine they shared his divine life and spirit. Thus was born comedy—the village songfest, a ritual for the decaying wintry days; tragedy—literally "goat song," the eating of the goat in communion with the god, an expression of the deepest pathos of Greek life. Gradually worshippers in the drama began to step out of the chorus onto the center of the stage as individual actors, and with that step we made the transition from choral to dialogic theater.

So early Greek plays developed as enactments of the myths of the gods, and religious festivals were simply dramatic contests involving the whole community. In Aeschylus, Sophocles, Euripides, Aristophanes, religions and theater were fused; a mirror held up to nature in such a way as to help man reflect on its meaning.

Why did early Christian leaders denounce the theater as thoroughly wicked? Witness Tertullian, Chrysostom, and Cyprian. The answer lies in the Roman innovation that theater be sheer "entertainment," that it be divested of serious intent. What had been an "incarnation of man's amazement" was now made functional for his amusement. So theater became circus and what was once a place to search for meaning in life became a place in which to escape from life.

De Gregoris points out that early religious drama (which is the substance of all drama) had two necessary characteristics.[12]

First, an audience *surrounded* the actors: "It is in the modern period that the theater became trapped in painted walls, the proscenium arch, and the darkened auditoriums." In the Elizabethan and Greek theaters the actors were surrounded, the stage open to the sky, and no walls. It was in this setting that man acted out his devastating crisis before his community. The crisis, then, of the spectators was not their enjoyment of the performance, but their exposure before existence.

Secondly, an altar of sacrifice was at the center of the stage. The actor was sacrificed on behalf of the participating audience. So in *Oedipus Rex* the king ripped out his eyes as religious sacrifice. It was no accident that when embryonic mystery plays were enacted in front of the cathedrals of Europe there mass was celebrated.

There is a third characteristic of "drama which is religious" which de Gregoris does not mention. Drama lives at the edge of Apollo and inevitably breaks out into orgy whenever men are successfully civilized. That is, the actors *surround* the *audience,* infiltrate the spectators and lead them off as roving bestial bands. Or rather, the audience *becomes* the actors.

The name of drama here is disguised as *Carnival* and is exclusively the phenomenon of cultured (ordered) countries. Primitive man lived on the edge of chaos and had no need of the third element, but Carnival erupts in history as the catharsis of denied subterranean impulses and their sensuous demand to be admitted into consciousness: Athens' Dionysian Revels, Rome's Saturnalia, Spain's Feast of Fools, Bavaria's Walpurgisnacht.

These outbursts cannot be suppressed. They appear in the gaps of all our legislation. The Feast of Fools, for example, was a Christian Carnival bursting out of the church's prohibition of theater— of bodily festival. Priests themselves took part, appearing in masks at mass, dressing up like women, even electing a Pope of Fools. And during the drunken celebration of the Eucharist they danced, threw dice, and sang lewd songs. It was finally condemned at the Council of Toledo in A.D. 635, but it is difficult to enforce legal sanction against libido. In 1444 at the Chapter of Sens, those who wanted to copulate during the mass were asked to at least go outside the church before coupling. "Doing it in the road" apparently is not all that new!

Our Christmas, April Fools' Day, and Mardi Gras are pale survivors of the daemonic buffoonery of the medieval cathedral: efforts to provide a guarded release for anarchic impulses.

Harold Ehrensberger a full generation ago called for the church to welcome back the prodigal (namely theater and dramatic expression) to its proper home. That suggestion has been followed by many with some success, most notably by Howard Moody's Judson Memorial Church in Greenwich Village. But it missed the point. I think rather that the church *is* the far country and consists wholly in prodigals down among the husks, that we must no longer expect the secular to come into the sacred, but that with high precedent of the gospel drama itself and the Christ-Happening, the sacred is nowhere *other* than in the secular. Most congregations have long since ceased to "surround" the actor-minister with genuine participation and empathy, and the minister himself has forgotten that the ritual, the sermon, the celebration, is an art form at the center of which is the sacrificial altar of personal love, and that he, like Oedipus Rex, should be willing to tear out his eyes that others might see. The Berrigan brothers, pouring blood on draft files, know what *Christian* drama really is and *where* it must play out its play. They tore out their freedom in order that we might be free to say: The war stops here.

But along with surrounding sacrifice we must also celebrate the antics of pure energy, of "sheer life" in "shocks of truth." To canonize sacrifice and repress earthy ebullience is to invite catastrophe. Alan McGlashan's picture of the soul of man as "the savage and beautiful country" is perfect. The two sides war, both primitive and ordered, like a country in civil struggle. And neither side must win. We must always *"fling in the world's face the Dionysian challenge—* life lived like a mountain torrent, sparkling and tumbling in the sunlight, carrying all life before it, crowned with beauty in the instant of its own destruction. . . ." For over against us stands forever the classic attitude:

> . . . marmoreal, calm, clear thinking; verbalized once and for all in
> the sonorous syllables of St. Augustine—PAX, ORDO, LEX, SOCIETAS:
> the four great pillars of Apollonian life.[13]

The Leaping Greenly Spirits of Trees

The early hippie movement might qualify as a "theater which is religious": a street drama to a dancing god, calling us back to "everything which is infinite, which is yes," reawakening our capacity for feeling, tempting us to open up our lives and let the sunshine in. We should have at least seen this meaning of the drug culture. It was in its highest moments a liturgy of participation that dramatically (illegality being an intensely theatrical mood) lifted up the anguish of living in an insensible culture. To be Greek about it—and perversely melodramatic—the kids tore out their minds that we might begin to feel again.

Ever since Homer, man has been warring for the ethic of glory (*The Iliad*) and voyaging for the adventure of identity (*The Odyssey*). The long history of politics is also the history of war with its development finally of the industrial society. The military mentality requires absolute obedience and subjugation of the self—the staccato steps of Patton before the infinite American flag should haunt us—in the same way that industrialization absolutely requires collectivizing. The middle class is produced by the need of the elite for a managerial space enclosing the proletariat. Thus the middle class becomes the great beneficiary of technocracy and at the same time gets locked in by the logic of its development: the technological extension of man shifts the center of gravity from the man to the extension.

You own a house. Then one day the house owns you, defines your life, and signals the end of your freedom. The industrial society has dramatically choked off my sense of movement and sensibility while technically exploding both. I can go anywhere and quickly, but to increase my movement I must lose myself. Now I am an automobile, now a spaceship. I have cables and gears, and beeping panels, and my exhaust is clouding my lungs. The price of technopolis is me, and that cost is even higher than *Playboy*.

Reason builds cities, belief organizes systems, symbols unfold in language, but if I am uniquely gifted as that creature capable of ecstasy, then *I have the ironic possibility of turning technology against itself* and wearing a badge with utter seriousness: better things for better living, through chemistry. Or rather, I refuse to take technology seriously by playing with it, turning *technics* into *fantasticks*.

If I cannot participate as person in the outer world, I can repose in the inner world (Middle-Earth). The scholastic vision took us up to God. The hippie dream took us in to God. The technocratic society simply took us in. Said San Francisco *Chronicle* columnist Charles McCabe:

> We live in a culture where it is fashionable, almost obligatory, to be on the take. Acquisition followed by affluence is the national ideal. We give, mostly, when we are forced by social pressures and company goals, and we damned well have in mind whether the gift is tax deductible.
>
> Yet most of us know there is something wrong with our way of life. The hippies look at their family, and see a mother with a neurosis and father with an ulcer, and they ask, Who needs it? [14]

There had to be a new space available in becoming human again, a new air to breathe. Drugs were actually very ancillary, trivial, and often dangerous to this sense of newness, except that without them many of us never would have been confronted by the new sensibility. Leary's interview in *Playboy* was heavily larded with sexual put-on—women feeling the vibrations of his "mythic potency" and such—but even *cum grano salis* he was right about our sensory deprivation.

> PLAYBOY: How about the sense of smell?
> LEARY: This is one of the most overwhelming aspects of an LSD experience. It seems as though for the first time you are breathing life, and you remember with amusement and distaste that plastic,

odorless, artificial gas that you used to consider air. During the LSD experience, you discover that you're actually inhaling an atmosphere composed of millions of microscopic strands of olfactory ticker tape, exploding in your nostrils with ecstatic meaning. When you sit across the room from a woman during an LSD session, you're aware of thousands of penetrating chemical messages floating from her through the air into your sensory center: a symphony of a thousand odors that all of us exude at every moment—the shampoo she uses, her cologne, her sweat, the exhaust and discharge from her digestive system, her sexual perfume, the fragrance of her clothing—grenades of eroticism exploding in the olfactory cell.[15]

Aldous Huxley—who appeared with Leary in Copenhagen discussing the relationship of drugs and religion, and who died of cancer the same day John F. Kennedy was shot—wrote with more restraint but with the same basic appreciation of the drug experience which opened "the doors of perception."

I took my pill at eleven. An hour and a half later, I was sitting in my study, looking intently at a small glass vase. The vase contained only three flowers—a full-blown Bell of Portugal rose, shell pink with a hint at every petal's base of a hotter, flamier hue; a large magenta and cream-colored carnation; and, pale purple at the end of its broken stalk, the bold heraldic blossom of an iris. Fortuitous and provisional, the little nosegay broke all the rules of traditional good taste. At breakfast that morning I had been struck by the lively dissonance of its colors. But that was no longer the point. I was not looking now at an unusual flower arrangement. I was seeing what Adam had seen on the morning of his creation—the miracle, moment by moment, of naked existence.[16]

There is no real point in diverting the issue by complaining that there is a qualitative difference between Huxley's experiment and the freak-outs down the block. Let us concede this distinction. Let us also concede that drug usage supports a brutalizing and virulent racket trading in human lives for profit, that hash in the ghetto is less soteriological than entrepreneurial. So *goddam* the pusher (whether he has French or CIA connections). But spare us the pious diatribe of a Diana Trilling who complains that Captain

America's transcendent trip from West to East in *Easy Rider* is financed by the sale of heroin. The *meaning* of the drug revolution for the American middle class of the sixties remains—and is clear. It was a call, however misguided or seductive, from the deeps of all that is human in us to reawaken to that sense of wonder that is our very *special* being.

There are very many who distrust hallucinogens for both good and bad reasons. If pot causes cancer or LSD disintegrates mental processes, then publicly label them lethal—though many of the same people who devoutly wish to keep them illegal are not so passionate in cleaning up the environment or rendering our highways safe. Certainly we don't *need* drugs any more than we *need* electric lights. But heightened sensory experience and expanded consciousness and a feeling of "cosmic" permission to live as historical men and women, that we cannot live without.

S. I. Hayakawa wrote a startling confirmation of this point in his foreword to *ETC*'s special issue on the psychedelic experience. Commenting on the quest for instant *satori,* the future president of San Francisco State said:

> But perhaps my basic reason for distrusting the dependence on "mind-expanding" drugs is that most people haven't learned to use the senses they possess. Speaking only for myself, I not only *hear* music; I *listen* to it when it is around, so that I find Muzak and other background music, intended to be heard but not listened to, utterly intolerable. When I am, in Carl Rogers' terms, open to my experience, I find the colors of the day, whether gray and foggy and muted or bright and sunlit, such vivid experiences that I sometimes pound my steering wheel with excitement. A neon-lit supermarket is often too much for me—so terribly rich in angles and color and dizzying perspectives that I must deliberately narrow my perceptions to the things on my grocery list lest I take forever to do the shopping. Paintings and sculptures and ceramics get me so intensely excited that I often come out of a museum higher than a kite. In short, I *use* my senses—at least some of them, some of the time. And I say, why disorient your beautiful senses with drugs and poisons before you have half discovered what they can do for you? [17]

Hayakawa, however, apparently preferred supermarket sensitivity to coalition with soul brothers at State. Community leaders of the famous strike (Dr. Charles Goodlet and Rev. A. Cecil Williams) reported that he often went to sleep during negotiation conferences with them. Well, I suppose we can't be receptive to everything, though it seems a pity to divide the world into neons and peons.

One recalls Emma Lazarus' famous invitation inscribed on Miss Liberty: "Give me your tired, your poor, your huddled masses yearning to breathe free. . . ." The underground press in Milwaukee exposited this with a new tag line: "This offer good except where voided by law." While Ferlinghetti was waiting for "the American eagle to straighten up and fly right," the counter-culture was making the world "safe for anarchy" by defying (ignoring!) all laws that prevented them from breaking free, from finding new spacious skies and leaping trees, from dreaming new dreams of peace. It is sad that most of this anarchy was unreflective, unformed, and ripe for paranoia—not to mention hepatitis. A smidgeon of homework would have shown that there is more to dreaming than just saying "wow!"

The American Dream Revisited

We may still help the cultures to understand one another by delineating a theme in Western history decisive for the American Dream. It is the utopian myth of the garden Paradise, with its consequence of the Fall, the devastation by sin, and the subsequent and unrelenting hope for the regaining of Paradise, the second Eden. And in counterpoint with this theme, the competing communities of the desert (the wilderness) and the technological society (the city).

The theme runs from the Genesis story all the way through the establishment of the National Park Service in the United States in 1890: from Adam to John Muir. The counterpoint runs from the Egyptian bondage and the Exodus, through the American urban revolution and the emergence of the secular city: from Moses to Harvey Cox, from Canaan to the Virgin Land. I shall briefly set the garden theme and then trace it to the American West.

The word *paradise* is a Greek adaptation of the Persian word for magnificent garden. It is used as Paradise only in the New Testament. In the Old Testament it literally means "park." The corresponding word in the Old Testament is *Eden,* which is to be translated "delight." Now this was not a literal garden, but a cosmological garden, much more serious than a literal garden, for this is a metaphysical delight, a Utopia where all is perfect.

This is a motivational Eden, a powerful and permanent vision. Inside the garden is paradise, a place of protection, fulfillment, peace, life, and innocence. Outside the garden is the wilderness, a place of testing deprivation, conflict, death, and guilt. The garden is placed eastward toward the sun, toward the future, toward promise, and fundamental to it is the image of the family, of community. The linchpin of Utopia is relationship, and the story of the Fall, therefore, is the story of the development of relationship. That is, paradise existed *before* woman, before confrontation with sexual energies. This does not mean that the perfect life is anti-sexual—or that bisexuality was a result of the Fall (Origen). It means only that paradise is crucially tested by the organization of multiple human demands.

There are four interlocking interpretations of the Fall that are illuminative for understanding Western man.

1. *The Fall as original sin.* Here the theme is quite obviously that the Fall was unfortunate, that it impinged on and destroyed Eden. The tree placed in the center of the garden means God's will and over against that man's will. The key to the retention of paradise then is submission to the other's will, and the garden story becomes a parable of obedience. The penalty for disobedience then is expulsion from the garden into the wilderness, the desert and death.

2. *The Fall as the myth of puberty.* In this interpretation the Fall is the story of maturation and it destroys Eden only by dramatizing the problem of community. The theme here is that the Fall was fortunate, a kind of fall upward, as Herbert Weisinger put it in *The Tragedy and Paradox of the Fortunate Fall.* Here the tree in the midst of the garden is the tree of knowledge, and in Hebrew "knowledge" is also the word for "intercourse," to *know* is to have

sexual relations with. The tempter is the serpent, the phallic symbol, the penis, and the penalty for the Fall is loss of innocence: that man should earn his living in the sweat of his face and that the woman should bear children. On this reading it is a parable of sexuality.

3. *The Fall as the drive to know.* Here the Fall is the story of urban life and it destroys Eden by ushering in the delights of the city, the possibility of the future. The theme of this third interpretation is that the Fall was fortunate, a kind of fall forward—for there is the constant drive to let the light shine. Knowledge here *means* knowledge. Have dominion, says the Lord God. Let there be light. Let there be no darkness at all. This, then, is a parable of possibility and on this reading the wilderness reverses its negative valence as man dominates and the city explodes: the urban paradise choking off our innocence. Then man begins to feel he must return to the desert as the place of spiritual preparation to restore the Edenic quality to the city. These were the monasteries in the wilderness. This was the Essene community by the Dead Sea so fatally attractive to James Pike. This was the purification of the people of God in the wilderness, the long wandering before the promised land, only then to return to conquer the walled cities with tested righteousness.

4. *The Fall as the story of unfaith.* Here original sin is the effort to categorize the world into good and evil. And the theme on this reading is that the Fall was unfortunate, that it was not so much a fall as an explosion into fragments. If you will pardon another painful pun, it was "Adamizing" the world. The source of this intriguing interpretation—the pun is mine—is Edward Hobbs. The "knowledge" of "good" and "evil" *splits* the world, and disallows any possibility of unity of the self with other self and with that world. Here the garden is the parable of alienation.

It is these interlocking interpretations of obedience, sexuality, possibility, and alienation, in counterpoint with the wilderness of death and refreshment, this garden vision, which leads Israel; and its dramatic cadence is the credo of the Old Testament and the New: the rhythm of Adam, the Fall, purification, paradise regained. The myth is repeated with Father Abraham as Adam, the bondage in Egypt as the Fall, the Exodus as the purification, and the gift of the land in Canaan as paradise regained. The myth is continued with Father David as Adam, the divided kingdom as the Fall, the prophets calling out of the wilderness excoriating the sin of the cities as the purification, and the reformation under Josiah as paradise regained. We see it again in Father Hezekiah as Adam, the Babylonian captivity as the Fall, the Ezra-Nehemiah reformation in the new temple and the codification of the law as the purification, and the messianic hope as paradise regained. It climaxes in Father Jesus as Adam, his rejection by his own people as the Fall, the crucifixion as purification, and the resurrection heralding paradise regained.

This mythic cadence—Eden, wilderness, Eden—is played out in the psyche of Western man, and becomes exceptionally powerful in the late Roman empire where the city is the wilderness and paradise is the city of God (Augustine). But the myth is ambiguous. At the climax of the development of ecumenical Christendom there is a vital question which has no answers: Is paradise *in* history or *beyond* it? Religious utopian communities ever since have reflected this ambiguity. Eden is both in and out of history. The Holy Roman Empire is both spiritual and political, and Pope Innocent III wields a two-edged sword. So also the "pursuit of the millennium" and the radical reformation.

It is against this background of the search for paradise and the rising tide in that search in the consciousness of England that one has to see John Milton's two great poems on paradise in 1667 and 1671. And it is also against the background that one sees the colonization of the New World. For even Christopher Columbus—assuming roundness—used Genesis 2:8 as part of his rationale for discovering. He could go to the garden eastward by sailing westward! It is written through all the Puritan records that America was the new Eden, a fact exquisitely documented by Henry Nash Smith (*Virgin Land*), R. W. B. Lewis (*The American Adam*), and Richard Van Alstyne (*The Genesis of American Nationalism*).

The church in the new world is the garden growing now in what has become a protective wilderness. The American Dream is the myth of the garden, a new innocence from the fall of European decadence. As the church communities became cities and the cities encroached on the purity of the Commonwealth, the myth drove men westward. America is *Shane,* a mobile prophet of the wilderness redeeming a new Eden of dirt farmers against the desert of cattlemen. America is the Mormons, finding a new promised land: a new Jordan River running down to the Dead Sea of the Great Salt Lake. This, they said, as they rode into the valley of Utah, is the place. America is the black man whose other-worldly vision translates into the Eden of this-worldly liberation, translates into the unutterable anguish of "Go down, Moses, down in Egypt land," into "Let my people go," into "deep river" and "come out the wilderness," into "come and go to that land." That translates into the Edenic grandiloquence of Martin Luther King: "I have a dream."

These rhythmic imperatives should keep even Dr. Hayakawa awake.

With this powerful theme in the American consciousness it was very natural that the communal protest began in middle-class enclaves in the city, attempting to turn them into asphalt Edens, and, failing that, went into diaspora—into the hills and plateaus of unpolluted promise where freedom seemed a possibility and where one could still *see* Jupiter aligned with Mars.

I said at the beginning of this chapter that the American myth and the Christian story were not the same. We can now see that the one is a degraded version of the other. But these harbingers of street theater masqueraded a soul that could reunite us with our own heritage. There was something deeply human in their frantic, formless escape from middle-American reality. We have co-opted their flight and music, trivialized their costumes and life-styles in a thousand vicious jokes, imprisoned their messiahs, invaded their catacombs. And as a kind of signal of our desperate fear dismissed their defenders in the academy as "fags"—the lineup, we are told in arch tones, being impressively homophile: Paul Goodman, Allen Ginsberg, Charles Reich, Martin Duberman, Malcolm Boyd, James Baldwin.

"Oh, Christ! I hate descending to such bullshitting rhetoric . . ."

wrote John Hersey to the Yale alumni, when trying to find the
"right words" to communicate "what extremity we have reached."
How *shall* we say it? There was an awakening there, a dawning
of an old truth, a rebirth of wonder. If the counter-culture was
stampeded into exile, crushed out by Apollonian inflexibility,
shot down like so many pagan predators by Joe America, tempted
to apathy by cynicism or silenced by despair, so much the worse
for the fulfillment of our dream. Real Christian love always
opened out onto the world, always put us in touch with our own
feelings and sensitized us to the other. The other was met as a
Thou. The baby Jesus, as the street people put it, shut our mouths
and opened our minds.

I am quite sure that a renaissance of receptivity is the last hope
we have. Charles Reich identifies the American crisis as the inability to act, and sees that crisis of powerlessness resolving
through the development of a new consciousness, a new total con-
figuration of our perceptions, which will transform our locked-in
organizational impersonality into full-bodied human beings again.
What he calls "revolution through consciousness" is very close to
what Ferlinghetti meant by "the rebirth of wonder," what e e cum-
mings rhapsodizes as "the leaping greenly spirits of trees." Says
Reich as he closes his own manifesto for a Dionysian ecology:

> For those who thought the world was irretrievably encased in metal
> and plastic and sterile stone, it seems a veritable greening of
> America.[18]

The heart of the crisis, however, is not in our inability to act,
but in our inability to love. Charles Reich's plastic world is Larry
McMurtry's movie machine. The picture show in Thalia, Texas,
has closed down, the Korean war is ending, and Sonny Crawford
is left with the void. America's technological genius has flickered
out and left a community of motionless celluloid. The American
Dream—that led from John Wayne's *Red River* adventure to
Ronald Reagan's patriotic *Storm Warning*—is over, left limp in
the streets by an insensate, tobacco-spitting trucker. The *Kid from
Texas* had a brief look at San Francisco's future and now lives in

a present that is forever past. He cannot love. His old coach's wife, who gave herself to him so often only to be used and exploited, now sees his emptiness and cries out:

> "I guess you thought I was so old and ugly you didn't owe me any explanations," she said. "You didn't need to be careful of me. . . . You didn't love me. Look at me, can't you even look at me!" [19]

There is this that the young have done for this country; by their popular culture, their metaphysics of marijuana, their protest, their songs and bizarre celebrations. They have said: Look at me, at yourselves—with all your picture shows, your imperial wisdom, your cyberculture. You didn't love me. And you didn't even love yourselves.

Our inability to love and to receive love—that is what hell is, said Seymour Glass in a "perfect day for banana fish," and Father Zosima before him to the brothers Karamazov. And John the Elder before him:

> He came to his own home and his own people received him not
> But to all who received him . . . he gave power. . . .[20]

6

Playing: The Resurrection
of the Body

How graceful are your feet in sandals,
O queenly maiden!
Your rounded thighs are like jewels, the
work of a master hand.
Your navel is a rounded bowl
that never lacks mixed wine.
Your belly is a heap of wheat,
encircled with lilies.
Your two breasts are like two fawns,
twins of a gazelle.

How fair and pleasant you are,
O loved one, delectable maiden!
You are stately as a palm tree,
and your breasts are like its clusters
of the vine,
and the scent of your breath like apples
and your kisses like the best wine
that goes down smoothly,
gliding over lips and teeth.

Song of Songs

Some say that ever against that season comes
Wherein our Saviour's birth is celebrated,

The bird of dawning singeth all night long:
And then, they say, no spirit dare stir abroad,
The nights are wholesome, then no planets strike,
No fairy tales, nor witch hath power to charm,
So hallowed and so gracious is the time.

MARCELLUS TO HORATIO
Hamlet

We need pray for no higher heaven than the pure senses can furnish, a purely sensuous life. Our present senses are but rudiments of what they are destined to become.

HENRY DAVID THOREAU
A Week on the Concord and Merrimack Rivers

Love Came Up at Christmas

So we come to love. Who among us knows what this is? The cybernetic tribe in *Hair* when announcing Aquarius sang of harmony and understanding, sympathy and truth abounding, and dreams of "golden living" visions.

> Then peace will guide the planets
> And love will steer the stars.*

What is this love? Not really the "responsible" love of internalized authority nor the measured eroticism of *Playboy*. It is more akin perhaps to the healthy curiosity of Lena, closer to Lars Gyllensten than Moses. It is an exorbitant search for touch, communal culture. It is more immersed in the blue waters of Camus' Mediterranean than blessed by any priest's agape.

Listen now as the young Camus celebrates the voluptuousness of life, a kind of baptism of sensuousness.

> Like a pebble made shiny by the tides, I was polished by the wind, worn down to the very soul. I was a bit of that force upon which I floated, then much of it, then all of it finally, merging the pulsings of my blood with the great sonorous beatings of that natural heart everpresent everywhere.

* Copyright © 1966 by Gerome Ragni and James Rado. Reprinted by permission of Pocket Books, Division of Simon & Schuster, Inc.

The sun is married to the sea, the vigorous body of youth delights in the fire of flesh. This is our single human gift.

Except the sun, kisses and wild perfumes, all seems futile to us. . . . There is but one love in this world—to embrace a woman's body is also to hold close to oneself that strange joy which descends from the sky to the sea. . . . There is no shame in being happy.[1]

In his notebooks of this same period in his life Camus was struck by the idea of a reversal of the story of Faust. Here a young man is promised by the devil all the goods of the world for twenty-four years, but the demonic price is not the boy's soul. It is his body. Camus comments that this price is high enough—and indeed our balcony jubilation would be ecstatic if we were to find in these circumstances that hell was full.

It is in fact a price we do not have to pay, any more than we must renew our subscription to *Playboy*. We have in the Jesus-Christ-Event an understanding of incarnation that allows—no, *insists*—that we receive our bodies as our own and that the consequent ecstasy springing out of such reception is the final affirmation of faith. To put it paraphrastically: if a man says he loves God and loves not his body, he is a liar, for God *is* bodily love.

Sam Keen underlined this point in *To a Dancing God* when he offered a new curriculum for Christian colleges which would include a course entitled "Introduction to Carnality." And Altizer said it plainly: "Orgasm is the only true worship." This is the moment in our history when we can finally be completely clear about our life-affirming faith. If the Christ-Happening means *anything,* it means that the *Word,* the creative energies, the possibilities for communion, the mystery of the multiverse, really became flesh.

This understanding of the Christian grace of sensuousness has been long aborning in me, but it burst in all its magnificence one December at the university at, of all things, a Christmas candle-light carol celebration. Even now it seems unbelievable that it actually took place. It has to be one of the most bizarrely redemptive stage accidents in the history of religious drama—though I am one of the few people who thought it had the remotest connection with salvation.

Every year the college set aside one Sunday night in December when all "living units" would march with lighted candles across the campus to the conservatory and sing carols, each unit being responsible for one special presentation. In the golden age of church-related piety (if there ever *was* such a time!) this was a proper and delicate occasion, full of disciplined Christmas courtesy. But as the campus became more secular in more desacralized times, most students thought it Mickey Mouse and treated it as a joke.

Now the senior music major in charge this particular mythic year, hoping to raise the general tone of the evening, found that Warren Kliewer, a professor of English at Earlham College and drama editor of *Mennonite Life,* had written a short, sophisticated and funny Christmas play based on an ancient song called "The Cherry Tree Carol." [2]

Kliewer's play is basically a conversation between a folk-singing angel (who announces that Mary is pregnant by God) and Joseph (a very suspicious, incredulous husband).[3] Mary appears twice, both times dancing, as the "Cherry Tree Carol" is sung at the beginning and at the end by the angel.

The scene opens with the arrival of the angel from heaven (lowered on a rope from the flies). She has a pack containing a variety of items, including a campstool, music stand, and a ukelele. She unpacks, sits on the stool (which has a defective leg), and sings:

> Joseph was an old man,
>   And an old man was he,
> When he wedded Mary
>   In the land of Galilee.
>
> Joseph and Mary walked
>   Through an orchard good,
> Where was cherries and berries
>   So red as any blood.

Joseph moves onto the stage, watching Mary dance, obviously un-
satisfied with Mary's explanation of the strange conception.

> ANGEL: Poor guy.
> (*Turning to audience.*)
> Well, what would you think?
> An old man with a beautiful young wife.
> I mean, you know, babies don't just happen:
> You don't just pick them off a cherry tree.
> Figure it out.

Joseph bumps into the angel as Mary dances off.

Now Joseph, as all would agree, is a carpenter, and Kliewer
provides him with a hammer in his workingman's apron. The point
of this prop is quite obviously to identify his trade and relate him
to the angel as a carpenter: he fixes her broken stool. In return
for this physical service, she provides some psychoanalytic service:
the angel takes on a Viennese accent and psychoanalyzes Joseph
while he reclines in the classic Freudian position.

> ANGEL: I see.
> (*She makes a note.*)
> Und, Meester Choseph, you are sure
> Zat zis inscrutable situation must
> Be cause by somezing natural—zat is,
> By some unnatural lust.

In order to relieve his anxiety, the angel sings and Mary dances
the last part of the carol, revealing the true nature of the child to
be, in both death and resurrection. Even so, as the angel leaves,
Joseph is left never knowing for sure.

This, then, was to be the climax of the Christmas candlelight
evening. It certainly was.

The actors selected for the play were a campus minister's wife
and a very popular young social science professor. Mary was to
be danced by a faculty wife. They had little time to rehearse,
arrange props, or really get control of the lines. There was no
dress rehearsal, but the angel did wear white and Joseph looked

like a carpenter. The college choir stood far to the back of the stage hidden by a screen of lights, ready to sing the concluding Christmas anthem. Thus the fullness of time.

This angel had no rope, so she just stepped out in *front* of the lights screening the choir. Her white dress promptly turned transparent to the entire student body, and being a most voluptuous woman she had instant attention. She sat down on a stool and for some reason put her pack somewhat behind her so that every time she reached for another item her dress, short and now translucent, rode well up on her substantial body. The audience was now beginning a kind of tentative convulsion.

The angel sang, but having forgotten to arrange for a microphone could not be heard over the rising appreciation for her posture. Mary danced, but she was as attractive as the angel and moved with such sensuous skill that she only compounded the excitement.

When Joseph finally appeared, his wide appeal won the cast some speaking space and the play moved on. But it was not to last. He was supposed to be a carpenter and in the evening's rush dropped his hammer head downward in the pocket of his apron, which made, of course, the handle stick straight up, quite phallic and quite noticed by everyone. When the angel said Kliewer's line as, "Hey, look at that. Is that a hammer?"—grabbing at it with some kind of primitive reflex, the place exploded in bedlam. If he had shouted in response, "No, you idiot, it's a screwdriver," the students would have run gibbering into the streets.

Somehow the play staggered on to the psychoanalytic scene. Joseph (who later absolutely swore he didn't know what was going on) still had his hammer in his apron as he lay down. As he leaned back, lo and behold, the hammer handle came up, stark straight in the air. The audience spasmed. He sat up, wondering (as he said) what was going wrong now. When he lay back down, the hammer rose again, majestically, triumphantly—the signal for a final hysteria.

Faculty stormed out, house mothers wept, students screamed with outraged delight. A university vice(!)-president reeled down the aisle, then hurried back in to drag his teen-age daughter out by the hand. Mary refused to reappear. Joseph and the angel mumbled some quick ending punctuated with inaudible references to fecal matter, and the choir sang—I swear it—"Lo, how a rose e'er blooming. From tender stem hath sprung!"

The campus rocked for weeks over that most famous of candle-light pageants. Even today it is a mark of distinction for some student to say in suitable hushed tones: I was *there*. One of the guardians of the campus virtue, an Episcopal priest by trade—are there any sensible Episcopal priests? There must be—expressed the dominant response in an indignant letter to the college newspaper.

Editor:
   I am writing this letter to you as an interested outsider who deals with the spiritual life of many of the UOP students.
   In another day I would have called the skit put on for students after the candle lighting on December 10th, "a sacrilege." To call something a sacrilege necessitates the belief in sacred things. Too many people today in the name of "freedom" are maligning holy things. After discussing the skit with many people my only conclusion is it was a vulgar display of bad manners.

At the height of the outrage another letter appeared mysteriously and was distributed across the campus, unsigned but open to all. It was cast in the form of a season's greetings and bore the title: "A Christmas Story: R.I.P. Cherry Tree."

   The spotlight defines a white figure, glowing in its whiteness, drag-ging a heavy-appearing sack across the stage. Suddenly the lights rise behind the white-clad figure, and we see it is a woman, we know it is a woman, flesh of our flesh, revealed in the crossfire of light that falls from above and rushes from behind. The hungry tigers growl, and we do not hear the song of the angel. A woman, draped in heavy skirt, moves with amazing grace, her dance depicts the words we cannot hear. The tigers growl, the kittens spit, and we do not see the dancer or the dance. A simple man enters stage right, the handle of a hammer thrusting from his apron pocket. But, oh, it is no hammer. It is most certainly not a hammer. It could not be a hammer. How absurd for a carpenter to carry a hammer in his apron! We know what it is, don't we! The tigers growl, the kittens purr, they spit, they close their eyes because they cannot bear to look upon a hammer. No one understands the man. No one sees the dance. No one hears the song of the angel.

We are convulsed. We are enraged. We are embarrassed. We are indignant. This is not the play we had expected. This is not the story we have had told to us for lo these many years. Who is putting us on, anyway? Who does the producer think we are, anyway? If he thinks we do not know what is going on he is utterly mistaken. We know who it is we expect. We know what it is we see. We know.

.   .   .   .

Oh, my children who are my brothers, who are my sisters. How bound we are to myths and symbols to communicate the meaning of our lives. (It was no hammer!) How bound we are in our humanity. (It was no hammer!) We are fixed fast in our flesh and our understanding of our flesh. (It was no hammer!) Here we are! Look at us, we who are the actors enacting our humanity in the darkness of the theater.

And the word became flesh . . . what a scandal!
    (Oh protecting wisdom of the virgin
    birth myth)
And the word became flesh . . . "God I thank
    thee that I am not like one of these . . ."
And the word became flesh . . . She brought
    forth—lying in a pile of straw . . . and
    laid Him in a manger.
And the word became flesh . . . "God, no . . ."
And the word became flesh . . . and dwelt among us.

Ah, what is that the angel says? "You think this poor man has trouble believing. What about yourselves?" Is that what she said? May the spirit of Emmanuel be with you.

It was all so theologically perfect, that "pornographic" Christmas pageant: celebrating conception with an erection! That was probably the *only* human Christmas play those students ever saw. Why is it so? Why have we allowed ourselves to be restricted to images of virginity, suffering, and death? We live in a *complete* world, a total experience. So where are the church's hymns to orgasm?

Surely the physical intimacies between men and women are not properly celebrated when they are "spiritualized." Flesh means suffering, but it means much more inclusively the rhythms of physical pleasure. We don't conceive children by parthenogenesis and it is a misreading of the intention of the Christian drama to pretend that holy men got born that way. Malcolm Boyd helped get himself dismissed from Wayne State University's campus ministry by suggesting over Detroit television that Jesus had a penis.[4] Boyd should have seen Joseph's hammer.

Even our play's accidental nature was appropriate, for the gospel of the Jesus-Christ-Event is always one of surprise. Edward Hobbs' interpretation of the Trinity is highly germane here. He translates "God" not only as the One beyond categories, but as the Limiter, that against which I know myself as creature and therefore not infinite. Jesus as the Christ is that event which exposes me as I really am, catches me off guard, or as Hobbs put it (without seeing our pageant!), "catches me with my pants down." The Spirit is that which brings us together, includes *all* in a vital unity. So the Father is Limiter, the Son is the Exposer, and the Spirit is the Includer.

And the Incarnation is therefore *never* predictable, marvelously capricious: art, if you will, in the making. We are met by grace in the most unexepected places. The Christian life when it is really lived *is* an adventure, and we never know when some combination of circumstances will reveal a deeper dimension of the human possibility. If it can happen at a candlelight Christmas pageant, it can happen anywhere.

So I call now for a new celebration of this Jesus-Christ-Event, this perspective of decision in human history that *requires* the actual resurrection of the body. I do not mean a surrogate body, or a vicarious body, or a celestial body. I mean *the* body, *my* body, which sweats and sleeps and shudders out in passion. This is no longer the time of the death of God, but indeed this is "the sun's birthday": I who was dead am alive again today.

And I call for a specifically "Christian" form of celebration, which ordinarily would be dismissed as unworthy of serious consideration and in fact quite pagan. It is as much an alternative to traditional worship as Mathews' rendering of the Christian Story is an alternative to the traditional transcendent Everyman-Christ. It may—it surely will—catch us with our pants down.

To Catch the Confidence of a King

We have paired off resisting and consuming, emptying and receiving. Our final movement in the journey of freedom is deciding. But what really follows from the radical decision to be human? The classic theological term is sanctification: making and being made holy. That translates as increase in love, growing up into the stature of the fullness of Christ, doing the truth in love.

But "love" is so ambiguously rich. It freights our deepest dreams about the quality of the Christian life. *All* the expositors make that clear. We have been told that there are three Greek words for love so often that *philia, eros,* and *agape* are practically transliterations. What word then must we have to lift up this Christian understanding of love?

Sharing? Yes, of course, but with too much residue of religiosity, too pious—as if I know I *ought* to share since I have so much to give.

Giving? Surely, but with too much smell of colonialism. I recognize you as weak, as in want, as suffering, and I come to you in mercy: fill your empty table with my fortunate goods, bind up your wounds and become the Samaritan. It is even noble. Or perhaps humble.

All this genre of words has the same slight suggestion of *goodness,* of bleeding-heart helpfulness, of vinyl charity, of a thinly disguised arrogance breeding just under the surface of "care." What we are reaching for here is wholeness, a kind of roundness, a word which "circles" love—a final clue to that compassion which would redeem even Mr. Sammler's planet.

Including? Close. As Captain Ahab said in the hushed harpooning boat, just before Moby Dick rose from the depths: "He is very near." Certainly we should be utterly inclusive as we expand our nonexploitative affection abroad. And that is a "deciding" correlate. Yet it misses the texture that we want, the *feel* of love, the freeing quality of love. Above all, it fails at the very heart of the issue we have been raising. It does not center us on the root ritual of a sensuous faith.

The word out of the paroxysm of Walpurgisnacht, that fills the void left by technocracy's usurpation of power and its gift of human leisure, that guarantees that my new Christian body will never be entangled again in the yoke of bondage, the word out of the silent night, is *play*.

It is still quite difficult for us to be "serious" about "play." The reason is that two different but honorable traditions have collided in America producing the most reprehensible life-style imaginable to the bourgeoisie: youth gone soft, undisciplined, and parasitical. The counter-culture does not fit the producer-consumer syndrome so necessary to a Madison Avenue world. Richard Nixon had to be sold to the nation in 1968: folded, packaged, and marketed on television and in the press and direct public appearances, had to become a plastic version of America's heartland—an efficient, highly mechanized Barry Goldwater. Make, display, compete, sell, consume, invest. This is the antiphony of capitalism, and the unforgivable sin in this "rhythm" system, just as in "Vatican roulette," is not to produce.

The first tradition is quite clear. He who does not work, let him not eat, said the Apostle Paul, John Calvin, John Smith, and George Wallace. This is the famous Protestant work ethic of R. H. Tawney. In *Religion and the Rise of Capitalism* he showed that Calvinism helped to prepare the soil in America for the harvest of good honest sweat. Salvation, to be sure, was by God's good grace and it would be impious of us to question it, save for a few minor fun questions such as whether man's original problem (read "sin") was supralapsarian or infralapsarian (read "games theologians play"). But one ought to write down the record of daily toil and review it carefully from time to sober time, since no man knew whether or not that grace had prefolded him into the kingdom. Ethical ledgers might come in handy as signs of a sort pointing toward righteousness. Redemption was a gift (as all knew), but industry had a certain celestial smell about it. "Good" still modified "works."

The second tradition has a slightly more catholic flavor to it and protests the fruits of the first, namely wealth. Wealth, it is claimed, may deflect a man from his proper spiritual discipline. The Jesus of the Gospel is made to talk incessantly and critically about money. Ruling isn't the problem, but rich ruling is. So very early the Christian church developed as one of its three virtues for the spiritually elite (priests and monks, and a nun or two) the vow of poverty. With humility and chastity as the other two, the actual record of the church leaders on all three was understandably none too good. But the vows certainly were impressive on paper, and anyway Augustine had saved the day by establishing that priestly authority and papal infallibility did not rest on impeccability.

So the tradition of clerical poverty grew and waxed incarnate in that paradigmatic hippie, St. Francis, whose name was given to the golden city of the American West and whose spirit was tuned in by the evanescent flower children. Those "children" drew affirmation from an unexpected source. Robert Theobald, British socioeconomist, advocate of the guaranteed annual wage, and featured along with Buckminster Fuller (*Utopia or Oblivion*) and Marshall McLuhan (*Understanding Media*) by Kendall College as a "living prophet" of the cyberculture, [5] is in fact quite sure that "work" is over. The problem for the future is not one of producing "jobs" at all, but creative artistic outlets for energies released but also untapped by technopolis. Computers, we are told, will police our cities, prepare our food, and release mankind once and for all from his servitude to survival. Thus many universities now are offering seminars on the new leisure. It is a future extremely difficult for most of us to imagine, but a strong confluence of scientific reports reinforce this predicted crisis of "free" time.

The hippies were way ahead on this one. One sweet young thing said to Harvey Cox in reply to his question as to where she got food: "But food just is!"

Food isn't, of course, in most of the world, as Paul Ehrlich will be glad to tell you (and hand you a do-it-yourself-zero-population kit—vasectomy is never having to say you're sorry), but seventy years ago there were no airplanes, thirty years ago there were no television systems, twenty years ago there was no Salk vaccine, and ten years ago there was no pill.

Perhaps day after tomorrow, by some miracle of ecological awareness, food *will* just be. Then the psychedelic path will lead over the bridge of cybernation; and with Herbert Marcuse as guru emeritus, Norman O. Brown as classicist in residence, and William F. Buckley, Jr., as anti-utopian court jester, we will establish the new-consciousness Camelot, telling the little ones tales of old Greenwich Village, the Haight, Millbrook, the Peanut Butter Conspiracy, of all the lotus-eating cadres of the leisure class. What will these leisure cadres do? Develop creative arts—like Ann Halprin's Avant-Garde Dancers' Workshop, like Luis Valdez's Teatro Campesino, like Howard Moody's Judson Theater, like Roger Ortmayer's environmental events, like Mary Corita's seriographic celebrations, like Sister Tina Bernal's ballet to God, like Peter Berg's "invisible circus" at Glide Memorial. The university could, in fact, become what it was: a *playground* and not a battleground. The church everywhere could be a happening where joy is like the rain.

For the hard-core Apollonians let me identify more precisely the classical source of my angle of vision. When the kingdom comes, Norman O. Brown will surely be at the right hand of our Lord, peeking cautiously under his seamless robe to see if it's not really Dionysus after all. I feel sure that Brown will report it accurately if he finds written on Jesus' jockey shorts that Malcolm was here.

Brown, of course, provides the subtitle for this final chapter and a set of fascinating footnotes on the importance of play. In *Life Against Death* we learn that an impressively diverse group of thinkers are struck by the centrality of play as a uniquely *human* function.[6]

Schiller's *Letters on the Aesthetic Education of Man* is cited by Brown and also forms the very heart of Herbert Read's theory on art education: "Man only plays when in the full meaning of the word he is a man, and he is only completely a man when he plays." Jean Paul Sartre from a slightly different angle agrees: "As soon as a man apprehends himself as free and wishes to use his freedom . . . then his activity is play." Johan Huizinga is called to witness that man is *homo ludens,* the playing man, and that there is an irreducible nonfunctional element of play in all the central human cultural activities: religion, art, war, economics, etc. In the civilizing process man has repressed that play element in order to allow for disciplined order to emerge. It is clear that civilization has dehumanized man if in fact play *is* so central.

The most intriguing witness, from my point of view, is the Protestant mystic theologian Jacob Boehme—not as advertised in Christian history as Calvin or Augustine, and for an obvious reason. He had the temerity to take the Christian promise of the resurrection of the flesh quite festively. The will, he said, was primary over the intellect. Since the essence of will is purposeful activity and activity is a result of need, then the only "activity" possible in a perfect state is "play." God's life itself for Boehme is "play," and we only express our lives to the fullest when we are playing.

Boehme in fact gives us a *fifth* interpretation of the Garden of Eden problem. Man was set in the garden by a playing God. To be disobedient was therefore *not* to play. *Adam fell when his "playing" became serious business!*

Freud used this same insight psychoanalytically. We have an unconscious desire, he tells us, to return to our childhood: to reenter paradise where our single activity is to pursue the pleasure of the body. The pressure of this desire is made more powerful by the reality principle that necessarily underlies our expanding culture. Civilization brings its discontents, which are factors that both alienate us from ourselves and sustain that civilization. That is why "work" is fundamentally "inhuman" (as Marx also correctly saw). The deepest desire we have therefore as human beings is to play, which is translated as that which overcomes alienation, estrangement—in Read's phrase: redeem the robot.

Now here is the final problem which Freud never solved and which I think sensuous Christianity does. The deepest longing we have is to return to freedom/pleasure, but this longing *must* be frustrated by maturity (the flaming sword). In other words, the child's experience of freedom has a fatal flaw: it cannot come to terms with death. Death is the final inhibitor of freedom and all other inhibitions grow out of our fear of death. God as Limiter is God as death. Fear of God means precisely this, and reveals why the first commandment is a non-negotiable demand. *That* is the reality principle. The child's world is manufactured out of the illusion of omni-freedom and survives into adulthood as fantasy and daydreams. The ultimate contradiction in the human person is between reality (Apollo-Death) and pleasure (Dionysus-Life). Freud saw no way to come to terms with death, and was honest enough to maintain a profound pessimism about the human condition.

Christian orthodoxy and some forms of Greek thought bypassed this problem formulated by Freud with the clever diversion of the "soul" as distinct from the body. Hedonists bypass the problem by covering it with surface sensuality, always terrified that tomorrow's exquisite pleasures may be numbed by advancing pain and ineptitude, subtly fearful of both frigidity and impotence, and contributing to both by Don Juan freneticism. Atheistic existentialists say no to death and do not go gently into that good night, but seal their center of loyalty to life within themselves and thus atomize their possibility for community (as in Hobbs' version of the Fall). Some physicists even reinterpret the age-old promise of immortality by cryogenics, and freeze Freud's problem for a future thaw in a triumphant utopia (as in Robert Ettinger's Michigan experiments). And of course there is the strategy of suppose indifference: in *2001* Lockwood's death, you will recall, is not even noticed.

The Jesus-Christ-Event looks at the problem straight on. No evasion, no façade. Death is not overcome, but it is used as the occasion to know life's finality, its utter and complete precariousness. *I die my death,* says Mathews. I pick it up and choose where I will thrust it in "the breach of history." *No man takes my life from me,* says Jesus the Christ. *I lay it down.*

In that moment we are passed from death into life, enabled to lay hold of all its ambiguities. This Christ-Happening exposes us, rips us untimely from the womb, holds unflinchingly before us the absurdity of thinking we were not born to die. As we receive this shock in faith we are born again: we reenter our childhood, reawaken our senses, our capacity for pleasure, begin a new sensitizing of our bodies both to ourselves and each other. In short, we are redeemed into play.

It must be understood that this playing man, this child-man, this Sensuous Christian, is human in a very special way. Our play is not simply a release into animal spontaneity which relaxes us from the arduous task of survival. Ernst Cassirer in his *Essay on Man* makes this point well enough. He sees, as Darwin, Huizinga, and even Freud did not, that play is not "a general organic activity but a specifically human one." Human play is "transcendental," not in the deflective sense of orthodox Christianity, but in the strictly phenomenological sense of what Kant called "the transcendental unity of apperception" (the miraculous ability of the cognitive function to range across our sensible experiences and unify them into perceptions which may then reenter the emotive life as a directional function: boy sees leg, arm, breast, face— thinks girl—acts like boy who has just seen girl). Cassirer goes on to draw a false conclusion concerning the distinction between a child's play and a mature artist's imagination, telling us that the child plays with things whereas the artist plays with forms (lines and designs, rhythms and melodies). Herbert Read picks up this false distinction and presses for a unity between child and man: that is, between sensuality and sensuousness.

> There is, in all free artistic activity in children, an instinctive activity of a formative nature, only distinct from a fully developed artistic activity in that its power of concentration is directed to the intelligible rather than the phenomenal world. The child gives intelligible form to its sensations and feelings rather than to its perceptions; but form it is; the imagination, as Schiller says, finally makes, in its attempt at a *free form,* the leap to aesthetic play! [7]

It is my thesis that the Christian gospel can only be understood as the aesthetic dimension of existence. The Sensuous Christian indeed makes a leap of faith, as Kierkegaard rightly said. But this faithfulness, having its genesis in the decision to shrug the world off our shoulders, as Ayn Rand rightly said (1,084 long pages—

she *is* serious!), is finally this leap into aesthetic play. Faith, therefore, is *a life of free form.*

Again, this is not chaos. It is not anarchy, not running off into the bush or worshipping at Walden, not degeneration of the mental faculties. It is particularly not the sophisticated slobbism of permissiveness.

It is rather the regeneration of the sensuous possibility of human persons. Schiller describes it perfectly:

A leap we must call it since a wholly new force now comes into play; for here, for the first time, the legislative faculty interferes with the operations of a blind instinct, subjects the arbitrary process of imagination to its immutable and eternal unity, imposes its own self-dependence upon the variable and its infiniteness upon the sensuous.[8]

And in a last burst of eloquence he sums up what I consider the Apostles' Creed of the Sensuous Christian:

In the midst of the awful realm of powers, and of the sacred realm of laws, the aesthetic creative impulse is building unawares a third joyous realm of play and of appearance, in which it releases mankind from all the shackles of circumstance and frees him from everything that may be called constraint, whether physical or moral. . . . *To grant freedom by means of freedom* is the fundamental law of this kingdom.[9]

Play, therefore, releases us from the burden of being "serious" about freedom. When we first see the world as turned over to us, realize that we *invent* meaning, we are tempted to think that value is only *in* ourselves. This is the existential condemnation, the exhaustion, the lonely individual floating off into final alienation on the ice flow of *Life* magazine. Play, on the contrary, uses the natural in a consciously "unnatural" way, breaks down the determinism of the cosmos, constructs a fun universe out of a serious polyverse. Play deprives the world of its "work" content, insists that nothing "good" comes from it. Play, by definition, rearranges the world without destroying the absolute intimacy between player and world. *What play consumes is receptivity, in exactly the same way that deciding rebels against emptiness.*

The Lord of the Dance

I have named this entire confessional a celebration of freedom and love and called for reaffirmation of the *body* of Christ, which is my *actual* body equipped with this miraculous possibility of free form in play. It is this essentially playful quality of the Christian which has been disguised by the church as "Christian love," misdirecting our attention by calling love "charity," "sharing," and "mercy," and litanizing it in the three Greek words.

Love is play. All children know this. Why does the square world of reality-stricken adults insist that it is not? To love someone is to *play* with them, dance with them, laugh with them, imagine with them, create with them. Just as poetry is play with words, language cut loose into new associations that provide what Walter Kerr calls "a shock of delight," so love is play with bodies, physical intimacy freed from old meanings and restraints, exploding into new shocks of delight. As Oscar Brown, Jr., sings in *Joy,* "It doesn't have to be such a *funky* world!"

Worship, then, for the Sensuous Christian is that activity which increases his sensitivity toward playful love. Most of the main-line churches I've seen are still bloated with normal, responsible, "mature" adults, who think they have grown up when they have just gotten dull. It has been a pathetic judgment on the church's misunderstanding of its nature that *sensitivity* groups had their origin outside its sponsorship. All churches should have become Esalen Institutes, where men and women (Bob and Carol and Ted and Alice) could have expanded their consciousness and developed *body* mysticism. We allowed that need to go unmet, tempted a generation of youth to believe that only a half-Martian like Michael Valentine (a stranger from a strange land) could teach earth's trusting creatures how to be water-brothers and bathe in each other's sensations.

Glide Memorial Church in San Francisco has powerfully challenged this evasive obscenity for years. It is one of the few *Chris-*

tian churches in this country and the period of its challenge exactly coincides with our axial time. Headed by Rev. Lewis Durham beginning in 1961, this amazing institution is an incarnation of Archie Hargreaves' call for a church as "a floating crap game," a community forming where the action is. It is a cauldron of body mystics and eschatological immanentalists—a ferocious gamble of frank embrace of the natural.

Glide formed the original Council of Religion and the Homosexual, founded on the assumption that homosexuality is not a disease but a *choice,* which has now inspired several all-homophile churches in the nation, as well as the Gay Liberation Front (with their buttons reading proudly "Queer Power"). Rev. Ted McIlvenna began the National Sex and Drug Forum there, a daring experiment in filtering sense out of all our fixated non-sense by exposing participants to concentrated *visual* sexual experience— all variety of graphically photographed activity projected simultaneously in marathon sessions to reinforce our fantasy life as healthy. Says McIlvenna: "Sex isn't good when it's responsible; it's only responsible when it's good!"

Such directness produces quite naturally a great deal of harassment by the government. Last year McIlvenna had over fifty of his films illegally confiscated by the FBI (*he* is protected by the educational privileges of the law) while he was a guest of the University of Minnesota School of Medicine, and where the faculty voted unanimously to include his program in their curriculum. When Constance Beeson filmed her evocation of sexuality from a woman's point of view entitled *The Unfolding,* its principals (Laird Sutton, Tess Wellborne) were from his staff and its premiere showing was in Glide's "Awareness Room." District attorneys and FBI agents have shown a remarkable attraction to its exciting triple imagining. Sutton has gone on to film a complete odyssey of sexual style, including intercourse among the paralyzed and exercises to cure premature ejaculation. Government guardians should be standing in line for this series! McIlvenna takes it all with just a tinge of growing cynicism, and passes out copies of *Eros Denied.*

Glide's "minister of celebration and involvement" is Hayakawa's old friend, the Rev. A. Cecil Williams, a tan classmate in 1952, who became black in 1963 and has helped transform Glide from a sepulcher into a sanctuary. He is the nearest approach to a Sensuous Minister that we have in our organized ranks (see *Playboy,* March 1972, "On the Scene"). Even his secretary is a spectacular entree into the world of sensuous ministering, with her mod dress, Asia-American imagination, and warm receptivity.

Williams, on a typical Sunday morning at Glide, undulates as the congregation (4,000 jammed in every week, most of them under twenty-five) sways and claps and sings songs of the street, of the movement, songs of joy, enveloped by soft folk jazz, driven by drums, and called into sensory awareness by lights and moving images projected completely across the front of the sanctuary. There is this steady pulsation to the service, as it builds its rhythms: now pausing in silence, now listening to a melodic chant ("Jesus is all right with me!"), now opening to the sermon—a lithe incantation of the contemporary—now climaxing with embrace, with bodies close and real, greeting one another with a kiss.

New? Of course not. It is a recovery of the genius of Christianity, which releases us to do for our own time, in our own way, what we must do to be human, and where the people really *are* glad to go into the house of the Lord.

There are many other awakenings to this need for worshipping play. St. Clement's Episcopal in New York had its communicants blindfolded, barefoot, and crawling a forty-minute maze over bread crumbs to the Holy Communion. One church printed instructions for charades on paper plates and sailed them into the congregation, where parishioners responded by acting them all out at once. Balloons, bright banners, dancing Snoopies, throbbing congo drums for living altar crucifixes, are all part of the new ecclesiastical décor.

One Lenten season we prepared for the resurrection of the body in a style more appropriate to our real bodies than the usual prescribed genuflections. We celebrated the five senses.

The first week was *taste,* so we invited the college food director to "preach" on tasting. After some hesitation, he got caught up in the spirit of the body (he was Jewish anyway and had a head start), even providing sacks of food for all the students who then ate as he talked. After showing slides of possible settings for maximum sensory enjoyment of the various foods we were eating, he asked the campus rabbi to sit with us at a table set for an evening meal. As we ate, the rabbi chatted gently about the tradition of *religious* appreciation that Jews have for food. Finishing with a goblet of wine, he passed the "chalice" over to us and as we paused to remember another night long ago, wondering how Christians could have ever allowed *hoc est corpus meum* to degenerate into *hocus pocus,* the choir—fully recovered from Christmas—sang softly:

> Bread of the world in mercy broken,
> Wine of the soul in mercy shed. . . .

For *touch* we were all blindfolded, and a blind student described to us her unfamiliar world of temperature, texture, shape, and motion. And D. H. Lawrence was called as a witness to our unease with "the messy intimacy" of pressing our bodies together.

Larry Walker shared his *vision* of receptivity to our environment: gave an invocation to experience. He showed us a motion picture of painting from a nude model, pointing out that pictures need not be a double remove from reality—it was for this reason, you will recall, that Plato banished artists from the perfect Republic—but that they are an enriched way of being real: they *demand* that we see.

Our Methodist chaplain used blindfolds again on us, as two dozen students walked trays of different *smells* under our noses, and at the climax of the service ignited great boxes of gunpowder, completely choking a crowd already stunned by recorded sounds of Vietnam.

Edgar Summerlin, composer of the famous jazz settings for Wesley's Order of Prayer, recorded with Roger Ortmayer, flew in from New York to let us *hear* some of the new sounds commissioned by the church. He even taught us to "sing" an instant hymn, composed by uttering ten different "spontaneous" sounds on signal, in various combinations, while he wandered about the sanctuary improvising a saxophone solo statement.

On Easter week we celebrated the *resurrection* itself, participating first in a condensed Reader's Theater version of *Who's Afraid*

of Virginia Woolf? All our senses ready, and with trim confidence
that we were human beings who tomorrow would be no more, we
began to dance. It started with a small circle of students behind
the altar pantomiming words sung by the blind girl.

"I danced in the morning when the world was begun,
And I danced in the moon and the stars and the sun,
And I came down from heaven and I danced on the earth,
At Bethlehem I had my birth.

"I danced on a Friday when the sky turned black,
It's hard to dance with the devil on your back,
They buried my body, they thought I'd gone,
But I am the Dance and I still go on.

"They cut me down and I leap up high,
I am the life that'll never, never die,
I'll live in you if you'll live in me,
I am the Lord of the Dance," said he.

Dance then wherever you may be,
"I am the Lord of the Dance," said he.
"And I'll lead you on wherever you may be,
And I'll lead you all in the dance," said he.*

Then that small circle broke, and to the words "leaped up high,"
they soared over the altar—leaps to stir the epinephrine of any
Nijinsky—into the congregation. Girls with baskets of flowers
scattered petals everywhere. The chapel organ picked up the
simple, irresistible melody, and to that crescendo of sound, the
altar ablaze with candles and incense, lights completely bright,
one by one the students embraced other students into the dance,
until at last the whole chapel was alive with motion and joy.

Dance then, wherever you may be.
"I am the Lord of the Dance," said he.

He really is.

* Copyright © 1963 by Galliard Ltd. All rights reserved. Used by permission of Galaxy Music Corp., N.Y., sole U.S. agent.

The Invisible Circus

If there are dangers in our first childhood, there are certainly exceeding dangers in our second. We must never be so romantic as to suppose that Dionysus cannot turn into Narcissus, or for that matter Ares. John Wesley, just after warming up his heart, warned that sanctification was a lifelong process rife with pitfalls and temptations for backsliding. My tradition informs me that I can fall from grace, and I believe it. When the bus moves out to Morgan Street I must make the decision *again* to pick up my life, and my playful rituals will continually remind me (expose to me) who I am.

There are two major dangers which imperil this perspective. The first is a failure to see the full implications of bodily play, and the second is the temptation to return to fascism. The first is a kind of myopia in utopia; the second is an ominous hint that play easily becomes "serious business." Our perspective is adolescent without sober recognition of these risks.

Concerning the first this much can be said quickly: It must not be assumed that celebrations have a necessary social conscience. Precisely the opposite. The "content" of our celebrations will depend on the hierarchy of *meanings* attached to the rituals. This, at least, is the way the person acculturated in the Western Christian tradition will most likely express his "play." He will give expression to a prior, almost "unconscious" moral structure. Typically he will dance instead of slitting his neighbor's throat. The dance, in other words, has content. What we want is for that content to be "good" (morally helpful, open, responsible as "capable of responding") without blocking our capacity for joy, curiosity, and wonder. We want our celebrations to be *both* ends in themselves (not *about* but *is*) *and* modes of solving the world's problems (food just isn't). There are dark ghettos, and one-crop economies, and the pale horse of famine rides on India's shoulder (it's hard to dance with the devil on your back). How does Sensuous Christianity address this crisis?

The answer to this question deserves more space—a full treatment actually of resurrection ethics; but the direction of such a treatment can be suggested here and developed briefly in the conclusion. The informing point has been stated tonically: Receiving our bodies *requires* us to take seriously not only "the Word made flesh," but also that "the earth is the Lord's and the fullness thereof." "Human" after all has its derivation from "humus," meaning "soil." If we must hold our gaze quite steadily and in a "spiritual" sense *exclusively* on this earth, then it follows that what happens anywhere in this world happens also to us. *I and my Father are one,* says the eschatological hero. *We are all one in Christ-Jesus,* affirms the Christian cultus. Translated into the twenty-first century, this means something beyond Feuerbach's "theology as anthropology." It means something radically inclusive (Hobbs' "Spirit"): *Theology has become ecology.*

Environmental disaster is a *religious* tragedy. Christendom always has held stewardship of resources as a virtue, but has managed to divert the absolute immediacy of that virtue by its straight and militant otherworldliness. The "land" was loved only as a staging ground for bigger (immortal) and better (holy) things through eschatology.

A resurrection-ethic makes this impossible. The world, as Luther said, is God's body, and if I know myself to be a body and one with the God as Jesus-Christ-Event, then my final commitment is to this *earth.* And at the *same* moment I dance out my joy at being alive, I also die my death for those whose lives are paralyzed by repression, hunger, ignorance, and transcendent fear. At the intersection of earth's need and my joy I lay down my life.

The central sacrament of the Christian cultus extrudes this commitment with theatrical genius. Our *Eucharist* is celebrated by eating and drinking and hearing the sensuous proclamation: This is my body and blood. It is earthy enough and to spare: a supper of bread and wine to affirm the one who died and lives. But there is this added richness of human intersection with the world's resources. Bread is *created* by man out of the natural. It does not come full grown—it is mixed, yeasted, and baked—then we eat it as body. So with wine: harvested, fermented, bottled—then we drink it as blood.

The point is, it is now our own body broken and our own blood poured out; for without us as creatures of earth there would be no banquet of God to share with the hungry of the world. Could there be a better ritual of reality, of deciding and playing, than this?

This, then, is the theological content of the ecological metaphor: God is that being whose circumference is nowhere and whose center is everywhere, the Vietnam war is being fought on the California coast, all wars are civil wars, earth is a finite island like my body, earth is my body.

Ecology is God: omnipresent, all things at once, who was and is and is to be, ubiquitous, total interrelatedness.

And God can die.

Then who will wipe the blood from us?

The second danger also needs an extended analysis, for it illustrates the fragile nature of bodily resurrection. At Glide, for example, Williams invited Peter Berg to create a celebration of human freedom. He called it "The Invisible Circus," and it consisted of a series of artistic testimonies to freedom (song, poetry, dance), with singularly imaginative polarities: films of U.S. planes bombing North Vietnam projected on one side of the sanctuary while belly dancers, naked from the waist up, writhed with abandon in front of the altar. It was all to take place on a Friday evening—high precedent this.

The spirit of free form was soon nothing but free. Play became positively vengeful. A woman stripped and danced on the altar, a man defecated on the organ (his gift to God, he explained), the ecstatic congregation began to copulate in the aisles, in the elevators, even on the roof (shades of *Marat/Sade*). When this last locale was reported to Berg, he remarked with obvious mock disgust: "What, on the roof! You mean out there under the stars!" *Carnival Redivivus.*

Word passed quickly in San Francisco that it was happening, baby, at Glide. Beginning with a mere four hundred, the crowd grew to five thousand (an historic figure!). Even the Hell's Angels —one might say *especially* the Hell's Angels—showed up for worship. Scheduled for one evening, the circus-*cum*-orgy lasted three days (perfect numerology for resurrections) since no Glide leader dared stop it lest the freaked-out communicants tear the building apart.

When it was over, Williams was in trouble. The media had been there to cover the Friday night celebration, but so brazen did the proceedings become that they all agreed not to print a line about the event. Bishop Donald Tippett, then head of Northern California Methodism, showed a lot of hard bark in the subsequent storm of criticism. This is an experimental church, he said, and experiments, if they *mean* anything real, can be dangerous. The old bishop knew about hazardous experiments. He once opened his church in New York City to conversation with the underworld and got an eye gouged out for his trouble. It sounds like something out of *Reader's Digest,* but the young gang member who maimed him later "got converted" and became an eye surgeon!

The closer we get to the center of the earth (the descent into hell) the more risk there is of red-hot explosions and quaking destruction. When explosions come they invite the repression that insures us against this destruction. The name of that insurance is naturally fascism. We have previously defined this as resubmission to a centralized authority in the pursuit of order in such a way as to allow the authority final control over all our freedoms. This tempting tyranny is always present on both sides of the interface of radical change. A fascist backlash for example is the raw recognition that change means change and not merely readjustment of identical stimuli. A fascist revolutionary cadre arising out of avant-garde political action is a hardening of the form of change into an ideology. So Camus in the quixotic fifties, and Carl Oglesby in the militant sixties, both warn that history must not be spelled with a capital H—human dialectic and ambiguity frozen into a melodramatic showdown with the cosmos. That, said Joshua/Jesus, is sweeping the room clean of one devil only to let in seven more.

The radical youth movement was perilously exposed at this point. At the famed Chicago convention of 1968, Middle America was shocked into awareness of that playful fringe on the edges of radical politics, named by Paul Krassner "Yippies" (the chimerical Youth International Party). These Yippies nominated "Pigasus" for president, and helped precipitate the "police riot" so graphically filmed in *Medium Cool* and *The Seasons Change*. The original plan at Chicago was to roast the pig and eat him as a communion rite. When the pig dies, so dies the Yippie, they said, and the *stated* purpose of the Yippie presence in Chicago was exactly that symbolic self-destruction. Paul Krassner actually presided over a funeral for the Yippie on a *Thursday!!*

But in 1969 when militants occupied the University of Chicago's administration building, the Yippies were back. Inside were the genuine, hard-core, *serious* student guerrillas. Outside was a group calling themselves the Chickenshits, too afraid to enter, parading their cowardice with yellow armbands, a yellow flag, and assembling to the martial music of kazoos. If they did crash into administrative meetings it was to bend minds with readings from *Catch-22*. Jerry Rubin reports that when they were refused their demands they left obsequiously, dropping to the floor and mumbling: "Grovel, grovel, grovel, who are we to ask for power?" (On to services at St. Clement's: who are we to ask for humble access!)

It made sense to try Tom Hayden for conspiracy. He was a straight, staid, brilliant, autocratic, male-chauvinist, radical strategist. But Jerry Rubin and Abbie Hoffman had no place in that trial (and Hayden openly resented their burlesque). They were clowns. Yippies. Dead, yet alive. Invisible circuses. The only court that could judge them was the youth culture laughmeter.

Yippies then were an aesthetic dimension of the radical revolution. Garry Wills' superb analysis of their "merry pranksterism," called "The Making of the Yippie Culture," is still instructive:

> Like Dadaists, Yippies represent the aesthetic side of a revolutionary movement. It was the custom to distinguish between "radicals" at the Chicago convention, and Yippies, and liberal McCarthy kids. The distinction is real, but partial—more a question of mood, of style, than of doctrinal divisions. In fact, the code of the Yippies is simply Castroism applied to art. Fidel's view of revolution is that

one acts and, through action, discovers the aims of revolution. Only by forswearing ideology—even the revolutionary ideology of Marx—does one discover radically new roles for society.

This is the approach of Dada to art: only by forswearing art does one open up to any new creative worlds. As Tristan Tzara puts it: "Thought is made in the mouth."

Our whole culture, Wills goes on to point out, is a kind of street theater, which mixes the "real" with the "representational." The aim is to show that there is no distinction (Ginsberg: there are no categories). Art gets free from art by destroying itself; or rather, what happens is that *everything* is turned into art (Op, Pop, Funk, Living Theater). The "idea" of rock concerts was to immerse oneself *completely* in undulating sound—allow the whole world to surround you, possess you. Strobe lights would disorient your normal perceptions and intrude a new look at the normally illuminated. *Hair* always opened with half the actors in the audience and finished with half the audience on the stage. Allan Kapro's "Happenings" and Ormayer's "Environmental Events" were all Dadaistic, playful efforts to return us to a loving relationship to the ordinary.

One particular "effect" used so much by the playful fringe happening and orgiastic drama deserves special mention, and that is *nudity,* for it is a strikingly pedagogical piece of street theater—one which on occasion has even attracted me. Desmond Morris claims that the ape is naked precisely *because* he is human. As the ape ran in the survival struggle he needed a natural air-conditioning system, which the smooth bare skin neatly provided in the flow of wind over sweat. But this "cooling system" was secondary, according to Morris. That smooth skin was also quite vulnerable, with its nerve endings on the surface. Thus man became the only animal that made his own clothes, which as technological extensions provided for his survival. Then clothes passed from protective to cultural to art—expressions of individuality (hand-made) and tribal identity (uniforms).

Now here is the overlooked point. Underneath all this cultural identity (clothes) is my skin, still with its nerve endings and fantastic sensibilities. My uniqueness as a human being, you will recall, is my capacity for ecstasy (Leary). Thus in order to renew my humanness I strip off my clothes. I am caressed, excited, exploded into a sensual heat, and have broken through a barrier which divides me from my environment. I am *one* with that environment, for I do not know where I stop and the earth starts (Mowry Baden). I am free. So the Cheyenne, says the Chief to Jack Crabb, are "human beings" because they know where "the center of the earth" is, know that the "whole earth is alive." The white man comes only to destroy, to burn, to kill. This is "the great burden of being white": he does not know that at the center of the earth "everything is alive." So the Bokononists in San Lorenzo (*Cat's Cradle*) practice that odd form of intercourse called *bokumaru,* where the lovers touch the soles of their feet together—a form outlawed under penalty of torturous death, of course, by the most Christian government. The white man destroys that world too, but not with fire—that would be too passionate. His grotesque technological genius freezes the earth with a frigid apocalyse called *ice-nine.* How whimsically right Vonnegut was to suggest that we try for one last contact with each other by pressing together the only part of our bodies which, despite all hooks and penalties and prohibitions, *must* still touch the earth.

But we are not free. There are laws *against* my stripping, against my uninhibited demonstrations of ecstasy. So my nudity becomes a protest against the present, looking to the future. Let me return to Wills for an incisive amplification:

> There is a combination of risk and challenge, of vulnerability and effrontery, in the act of public nudity that makes it a natural experiment for a culture that is, precisely, devoted to performing experiments on itself, testing its own reactions, trying everything out. Nudes often appeared in Happenings. Then nudity (as opposed to *Playboy*'s pastry base breasts) spread through the underground press, where it was often used as a political weapon. Finally, it went onto the street in "guerrilla theatre" performances and demonstrations—first on the West Coast, then at the Chicago convention and in New York, as well as at the Washington Inauguration. Significantly, nudity first made a timid appearance on Broadway as part of a simulated "Be-In" by the young cast of *Hair.*

174   *The Sensuous Christian*

Terrence McNally was not so timid. In his 1968 play *Sweet Eros,* he presented what Wills describes as "nudity as a human experiment." A deranged man ties a girl in a chair, undresses her, and studies her with a magnifying glass, as if she were an insect or a lab specimen. Her nudity makes her into a prop: an object for both actor and audience to use. Only as the novelty wears off for the spectators is she allowed to move or react, to become a character—to be humanized rather than remain part of the decor. Thus McNally's play was an experiment performed on the audience: to see if it could overcome raw distraction and allow the girl to become another person in the story.

This "playing" with nakedness is part of our growth into love. The disrobing of a partner in intimacy in the consumer stage is competitive (how far can I go?). In the second stage we are naked to "receive" each other. In the last stage we advance beyond all inhibitions and participate fully in one another. It is a sharing and a giving—and occasionally even charity! But it is finally free-form play. Richard Underwood once hinted at this in a vastly subterranean pun. Nudity, he said, is not *scatological,* it is *eschatological.*[10]

I wrote at the beginning of this section of danger, of invisible circuses, Yippies, esoteric religious cults, sensitivity laboratories, of a culture rolling stoned. This insanity will not in its present formlessness yield a new consciousness. It may in fact teach us, as Buckley comments, "how to destroy our lives with a little help from our friends." That "greening" will wither and die unless its roots go deep into some sensuous *theology* that will give it nourishment and shape its foliation. April also exposes a great deal of decay.

Exotic life-styles, legal drugs, new mysticism, astrological charts, communes and four-way marriages, electric music, crazies in the streets and hippies in the hills—these are not enough. They are signs and portents that we are not *willingly* sick, but any experimental counter-culture will escalate its protest until beauty passes into orgy and sit-ins into violence. At this point, when the seismograph jumps wildly, those in the death culture (competition, consumerism, priority of property over persons, Apollonian fanatics of order) will react to the now evident threat of total change with excruciating impositions of structure. A particularly insidious reaction will be disguised as tolerant compromise: let the "kids" gather on the hillsides, allow them just enough freedom for their music to become electronic barbed wire, lower the visibility of the war in Vietnam (change the color of the bodies), let them vote. See how quiet they become.

And those in the life culture (communal life-styles, cooperation with nature, priority of persons over property, Dionysian communicants) have their own fatal weakness. They still seek to bring in the new age by idealizing the future and caressing it with the past. They still seek a Messiah: Che is canonized; Castro is "more in touch with himself than any man alive"; Mao's little red wisdom has made China into the new Eden; look—over the great youth movement—it's Ho Chi Minh Superstar. Let the new culture apply their own word to this Mickey Maoism: Bullshit.

Peter Gay's chilling description of German youth in the late twenties should be a warning to us all that there is more than one way to satisfy the thirst for freedom and love.

> But all *Wandervogel* except the most casual attached an enormous importance to their movement, an importance dimly felt but fervently articulated; as solemn, rebellious bourgeois—and they were nearly all bourgeois—they saw their rambling, their singing, their huddling around the campfire, their visits to venerable ruins, as haven from a Germany they could not respect or even understand, as an experiment in restoring primitive bonds that overwhelming events and insidious forces had loosened or destroyed—in a word, as a critique of the adult world. . . . The *Wandervogel* sought warmth and comradeliness, an escape from the lies spawned by petty bourgeois culture, a clean way of life unmarked by the use of alcohol or tobacco. . . . The result was a peculiarly undoctrinaire, unanalytical, in fact unpolitical socialism—Everywhere, amid endless splintering of groups and futile efforts at reunion, there was a certain fixation on the experience of youth itself. . . . Flight into the future through flight into the past, reformation through nostalgia—in the end, such thinking amounted to nothing more than the decision to make adolescence itself into an ideology. . . . The hunger for wholeness was awash with hate; the political, and sometimes the private,

world of its chief spokesman was a paranoid world, filled with ene-mies; the dehumanizing machine, capitalist materialism, godless rationalism, rootless society, cosmopolitan Jews, and that all-devour-ing monster, the city.

As Wills goes on to remind us, all the needs of the society were soon met. The celebration of the new man by the youth cult would last a thousand years. They rallied together in great festivals, and the need to shock became state terrorism. The old discarded myths were replaced by the Master Race. Wills offers this stinging con-clusion: "Community became the invincible *Volk*. And violence was *Blitzkrieg*." It was, as the kids say, "Beautiful."

In a contemplative moment such as this we ought to count the cost of loving revolution, take account of our arrogance, and look once more for some clue, some legitimate transcendence that might cut through our narcissism and strike through the mass of our idolatries. Tyranny is too high and too unnecessary a price to pay for free decision atomized and love's body prostituted. Adolf Hitler kept his campaign promises to stop the students from rioting in the street and to restore law and order and decency to the nation. He did indeed bring the Germans together.

Conclusion: I Am Serious, Greening

Deepest in the thicket, thorns spell a word,   20
Born laughing, I've believed in the Absurd,
Which brought me this far; henceforth, if I can,   20
I must impersonate a serious man.

JOHN UPDIKE
From *Midpoint and Other Poems* by John Updike. Copyright © 1963, 1969 by John Updike. Reprinted by permission of Alfred A. Knopf, Inc.

"But there was one sentence they kept coming to again and again in the loyalty hearing," sighed Minton. " 'Americans,' " he said, quoting his wife's letter to the *Times*, " 'are forever searching for love in forms it never takes, in places it can never be. It must have something to do with the vanished frontier.' "

HORLICK MINTON IN KURT VONNEGUT, JR.
Cat's Cradle

Of all the worn, smudged, dog's-eared words in our vocabulary, "love" is surely the grubbiest, smelliest, slimiest. Bawled from a million pulpits, lasciviously crooned through hundreds of millions of loud-speakers, it has become an outrage to good taste and decent feeling, an obscenity which one hesitates to pronounce. And yet it has to be pronounced, for, after all, Love is the last word.

ALDOUS HUXLEY
Tomorrow and Tomorrow and Tomorrow

There is this residual haunting question that still unsettles these ordered fantasies of mine, the problem that no one can solve and no one can avoid: the irreducible reality of the clash of value stances. *Who* determines value?

I do, of course. But my clumsy files are stuffed with a hundred intelligent alternative styles of being. I have interviewed the world, locked the church, watched the wake for "God," picked up my life, eaten the plastic fruits of technocracy, been raped by the infinite, and played on the edges of revolution.

Still this question will not down. It may be that I am suffering from a dormant plague, stirred up by dancing feet in Morgan Street. The question is ontological.

At Albion one of the most revered landmarks was a rock (five tons of it) in the quadrangle. The students there painted the rock—reflective of the seasons, holiday moods, the latest political crises, the campus happenings. Often the painting would slop over to the sidewalk where students took the opportunity to add sophomoric slogans such as "Virginity causes cancer," or even more socially conscious graffiti like "Use contraceptives: no deposit, no return." One year the administration ordered the rock moved, and it was, by five (easy?) pieces of machinery, off its historic resting place to a spot some twenty-five feet away. But the students revolted and under cover of darkness buried it with a sign over the fresh grave: "In three days the Rock will rise again." And it did—restored to its former place on the main sidewalk—with the aid of ropes, two hundred captive freshmen, and books on Egyptian pyramid building. They even built a kind of altar around it and cemented it in. If the administration wanted it moved again they would have to blast it off. The campus religious council held a wry vesper service around the rock, dedicated it, all to the syncopated chants of "Rock-a-My-Soul" and "I Shall Not Be Moved."

Collegiate silliness? Respect for tradition? Certainly nothing profound. But what if the rock had become a growing stone, a symbol at Albion of stability? When all else was shifting—ideas, values, faculty, administration, physical plant—could it have been that the students unconsciously sought a symbol of something that does not change: something solid, sure, something granitic: a transcending rock?

We could turn to any one of a dozen serious efforts to show the disturbing power of this quest as it probes behind our subjective affirmations. I want to bring forward two last witnesses, both of whom converge at a remarkably fundamental point.

Paul Tillich was my teacher as well as Altizer's. In his most trenchant study of the problem of competing values he wrote:

> One cannot discuss the ontological foundations of love, power, and justice without presupposing their ethical functions, and one cannot discuss their ethical functions without referring constantly to their ontological foundations.
>
> Ethics is the science of man's moral existence, asking for the roots of the moral imperative, the criteria of its validity, the sources of its contents, the forces of its realization. . . . There is no answer in ethics without an explicit or implicit assertion about the nature of being.[1]

Tillich's own way of formulating the alternatives to the pressure of the ontological question is a well-known triad: autonomy (values as self-authenticating), heteronomy (values as impressed by some form of culture, including bibliolatry), and theonomy. Theonomy is one of Tillich's more ambiguous words, in a vocabulary of studied, towering, disciplined ambiguity, but what he appears to mean is that man comes to a mystic awareness, a sensitivity to the ground of being, a finite transcendence of our self-estrangement by the unique relationship to the claims of the holy upon us that renders possible all relationships whatsoever. All ethics grow out of this relationship. He summarizes: "Every valid ethical commandment is an expression of man's essential relation to himself, to others, and to the universe." [2]

Ontology, of course, presupposes some form of revelation, since being *qua* being could not be known unless being presents itself, gives itself, at least in possibility. Even if reason be exercised to discover the nature of being, the rational life only operates within the structure of being itself and is therefore limited to the power of being. Thus when Tillich says that revelation is *reason in ecstasy,* and that love is *justice in ecstasy,* he is pointing to the mystical ground of all relationships and in Christian terms to the grace of God.

From a more existentially informed and consciously nonsystematic, but nonetheless ontological frame of reference, H. Richard Niebuhr makes the same point. "Radical monotheism," he wrote, "dethrones all absolutes short of the principle of being itself. At the same time it reverences every relative existence. Its two great mottoes are: 'I am the Lord thy God, thou shalt have no other gods before me' and 'Whatever is, is good.' "³

In Niebuhr, Tillich's three choices become henotheism, polytheism, and monotheism—and no one escapes one of these choices with its ultimate suffix. Gods are gods of faith, which means value centers and concerns, and all men are therefore "godists," theists, believers—however "temporary." It remains the task of serious reflection to determine which "god" is more appropriate to "whatever is." So Niebuhr pushes our neutrality: "To deny the reality of a supernatural being called 'God' is one thing; to live without confidence in some center of value and without loyalty to a cause is another."⁴

Henotheism means one god among many regnant for a particular community, and corresponds roughly to heteronomy. Our standards here are derived from the community! we are judged by that society and that society transcends us, goes on when we do not. This god is a collective noun representing the community ethos and the ideals of that ethos are imposed on us by the society. Religiously speaking this is nationalism, and we are well aware of its power to command ethical strategy—as in the German "solution" to the Jewish "problem." What *made* the Jews a problem was their ancient refusal to accommodate to the local tribal god. Amos would have been an unlikely candidate for either the *Volkskirche* or the *Wehrmacht*.

Polytheism is the benefactor of shattered henotheism, and is again vaguely equivalent to Tillich's autonomous alternative. When confidence in a nation, the church, the scientific community, the family, the American Dream, begins to wane, when the garnished house of heteronomy is unoccupied, then come the seven devils, the multiple centers of values, scattered loyalties. "When the half-gods go the minimal gods arrive." This breakup can be bitter, even nauseous, when suddenly the authority is gone, or called into question by observation of nonintegrity, by manipulation of power, by undue intimacy with the educational system, by patently superior glories and visions that intrude on our naïvete. Then men turn to isolated selfhood; to epicureanism, where the self seeks to organize its activities around a pleasurable state of feeling, a "dual sentiency" where all values and dis-values depend on insulation from pain; to existentialism, where the self seeks its confidence not in the self but of a self, confident in nothing, but nevertheless projecting toward nothing. And when men can no longer bear this isolation they give it away in pluralism where one achieves his sense of value by how he is valued by a variety of persons, communities, cultures. Like a metaphysical Don Juan this isolated man has many transient love affairs with each center, all in the desperate search to establish his worth.

Niebuhr cites Aristophanes: "Whirl is King, having driven out Zeus." The isolated man whirls from one value to another. Zeus is now truth, now beauty, now justice, now love, now goodness. Zeus is science as curiosity, art as the urge to make, politics as the will to power. Zeus is established religion, the academic community, a member of the arts.

Modern man is no different. He wants power, wealth, love, truth, beauty—but cannot pursue them all and no longer has any means of deciding which he shall desire the most.

Niebuhr found his "means of deciding," his rock, his stability (where his student, Joseph Mathews, also found his), in *radical monotheism.*

For radical monotheism the value-center is neither closed society nor the principle of such a society but the principle of being itself; its reference is to no one reality among the many but to One beyond all the many, whence all the many derive their being, and by participation in which they exist. As faith, it is reliance on the source of all being for the significance of the self and of all that exists. It is the assurance that because I am, I am valued, and because you are, you are beloved, and because whatever is has being, therefore it is worthy of love. It is the confidence that whatever is, is good, because it exists as one thing among the many which all have their origin and their being in the One—the principle of being which is also the principle of value. In Him we live and move and have our being not only as existent but as worthy of existence and worthy in existence. It is not a relation to any finite, natural, or supernatural, value-center that confers value on self and some of its companions in being, but it is value relation to the One to whom all is being related.[5]

It is this "ontology of ethics" that finally cuts through our problem by changing the question we ask ourselves in the pilgrimage of freedom from "Who am I?" and "What does it all mean?" to "What is going on?" This "ontology" intersects all the possible answers to the question of oughtness by affirming the very basis of the question. Freedom then becomes not something we invent, but our being itself: it is transcendent freedom, the *urfreedom,* grounded in the One who is not one among many, but One who *is* the many. Freedom is not an absolute from which we can extrapolate "God." Sartre's professor in *The Age of Reason* waited all his life for freedom to be *granted* him: relating, reacting, but never committing, never biting—and he had just noticed that all his teeth were gone. He needn't have waited: he *was* freedom.

The questions are changed. "Who am I?" is asked out of heteronomy, and the resisting man drives forward into autonomy where he comes among the husks of anomie, of emptiness, and wants now to know "What does it all mean?" As he comes to himself, he lays hold of the world as actual earth with his bondage over and his interest infinite, theonomous: "What is going on?"

And this free being is *not* capitulating to hope beyond history. He is not affirming the sacredness of human personality. He is, to reach for one more epigram, *affirming the humanness of sacred personality.* His emancipation is not vaporized into spirit, but is thrust forward through his body in protest against a parochial henotheistic identification, spreads widely (even wildly) through all the polytrophic sensitivities earth provides, coming at last into loving wholeness—marked as utterly unique by ecstatic union and playful compassion. There are then no longer questions but confessions: *I am my body; I receive the world through my body as a gift; I have decided to love.*

I am well aware that this may look like a relapse into van Buren's "ontological hangover," that it puts me in the evasive position of seeming to accept revelation, but let me quickly define what I mean by revelation. It is not revelation as *communication* where the spirit would send signals to be picked up by the sensitive instruments of human receptivity (Chad Walsh), though weird connections are reported daily by devotees of exotic meditations. It is not revelation as *information* where extrapolations are made from sensory evidence to value probabilities (Julian Huxley), though some careful prepositioning invites respect and even romantic affirmation. It is not revelation only as *insight* where latent images suddenly cohere in a pattern of meaning (Bernard Lonergan), though such conditioned ecstasy is part of what I do mean in the sense that art is revelatory.

I mean precisely revelation as *perspective* where some powerful historical event has focused the way we look at life so decisively that all our values are drawn out of that event. It is revelation as the appeal to that direct intuition of special occasions. It is what Fuchs lifts up as *Sprache,* a speech-event so moving that now we speak not in order to be understood but because we *are* understood. It is a self so richly liking another self that he bursts out of apathy into the triumphant "Elaine." It is D'Arrast carrying the stone to the native hut. It is Lena feeling the presence of Martin Luther King. It is Eldridge Cleaver realizing he is not a Negro. It is Mario Savio throwing himself on the wheels of multiversity. It is Tim Leary's fevered brain and Cecil Williams' incantations. It is candlelight hysteria and a blind girl helping us to see. It is nakedness in the clear Athenian air.

Huston Smith once suggested that a theological perspective is like wearing a pair of glasses. The glasses determine our focus on the world and every rule is read by their refraction. The glasses may be changed, freshly ground, or strengthened, but no one is without a pair. Sometimes after they have been on our noses for a long time, we forget that they *are* there, and begin to claim that we see with unbiased, empirical, intuitive, or revealed vision. Then our particular focus freezes into a normative perspective which we insist should be everywhere the same. In philosophy this is *absolutism,* in the natural world *scientism,* in education *authoritar-*

ianism, in theology *dogmatism* and in terms of human personality produces a jumble of jackasses each braying that they alone possess the path to truth and calling all the rest intellectual thumb-suckers.

This is my pair of lenses, freedom and love. By *freedom* I mean the stunning realization that we may say yes to our own history without saying no to the world. By *love* I mean playing out that yes as a totally unashamed sensuous being. It is vision refracted through the story of Joshua of Nazareth whom men made Jesus the Christ as a radical inversion of transcendent hope. The illuminating event, the Word made flesh that makes relationship possible, remains the Jesus-Christ-Event. It was revealed to me. I did not invent it, though it may have been invented. I heard it proclaimed. I see it lived out. Being itself was said to be flesh, that is the Word, the speech-event by which I know myself to be understood. That is, I am valued; that is, I am loved. And that love comes to me as totally and openly human, incarnated in a few men and women who have accepted me, touched me, and let me be alive.

The trustees of this perspective have been called the Christian Church and their high mediation of this ontological history of love has been carried in some of history's most barbarous trivialities, but that biform symbol is *my* reality out of which I love and I am loved.

Camus once wrote that man is the only creature who refuses to be what he is. At last we can confess that redemption from this tragic refusal is to distinguish between meaning and purpose. We rightly refuse to live without meaning. But we also hold as a sacred trust that life has no purpose at all. It means what we make it mean. Isn't it time to come completely clean about this, once for all?

What fine flustards we are, staring dumbly at the sky, waiting for things that will never come by.

Why wait another day to be what we are?

Notes

CHAPTER 1

1. *Cf.* Philip Slater, *The Pursuit of Loneliness: American Culture at the Breaking Point* (Boston: Beacon Press, 1970), pp. 59–60, where he calls Mrs. Robinson an "absolutely open" vampire, and enlarges the symbolism of the cross to include the young warding off parents who *feed* on the accomplishments and energy of their children: "She wants only to feed on his youth and obtain sexual gratification from him. . . . The cross, then, is necessary to ward off the elders, whose vampiresque involvement with the hero has been insufficiently exorcised."

2. (San Francisco: Jossey-Bass, 1968.) Four years of investigation of the leaders of the FSM compels Katz to conclude that they were quite typically "ideal" student types: high achievers, socially and morally responsible, and intellectually superior—precisely what every respectable Admissions Office is looking for.

3. *Atlantic Monthly*, November, 1965, p. 119; published in book form as part of *The Troubled Campus* (Boston: Little Brown, 1966), with an introduction to the entire collection by Edward A. Weeks.

4. Quoted in *Saturday Review*, January 16, 1965, p. 66.

5. Wallace Hamilton, *The Thunder of Bare Feet* (Old Tappan, N.J.: Fleming H. Revell and Company, 1964), p. 151.

6. *Pacific Review*, Winter, 1965–66, Bulletin of the University of the Pacific, Vol. 54, No. 1, February, 1966, pp. 4–5.

7. Paul Tillich, *The New Being* (New York: Scribner's, 1955), pp. 107–108.

8. *Ibid.*, pp. 108–109.

9. *Cf.* Slater, *op. cit.*, p. 59, on the natural use of the cross as a

symbol of rebellion: "But to young Christian activists it was not shocking at all, but a proper role for the cross to play. For was not Jesus himself impatient with traditional forms and rude to authority? Can it not be said of him that he acted in bad taste, and refused to seek reform through proper channels? Wasn't throwing the money changers out of the Temple a far more obstreperous act than occupying a building? But then Jesus was very much a Yippie, which is why he wound up in jail, Jerusalem being the Chicago of its day."

10. *The New York University Alumni News,* May, 1968.

11. As a matter of fact, later we did have the "high priest" of the Satanic Church, Anton LeVey, without a stir from the public. But we brought him without publicity and very late at night! The students jammed the chapel anyway, thinking I suppose that he would, in good witchcraft style, sacrifice a nude virgin on the altar. From any campus survey I have seen, witchcraft will have to find another way to worship.

12. Theodore Roszak somewhat cynically points out that Leary's first psychedelic celebration was held in September of 1966, just six months after his lawyer had appealed one of Leary's narcotics convictions as a violation of religious freedom. That would not place Leary as the first man ever to use religion as a legal insulation, but in fact Roszak's point is at least irrelevant (as he admits), and certainly misleading. If Marx stood Hegel on his feet, then Leary turned Marx inside out, making "opiate" the religion of the people! See *The Making of a Counter Culture* (Garden City, New York: Doubleday and Sons, 1969), p. 165.

13. Timothy Leary, *The Politics of Ecstasy* (New York: College Notes and Texts, Inc., 1968), pp. 56–57. The printed version is only slightly altered from the speech: "expert" for "spiritual advisor," and "mundane" for "secular." See Timothy Leary and Walter Houston Clark, "Religious Implications of Consciousness Changing Drugs," *Religious Education,* May–June, 1963, Vol. LVIII, No. 3, pp. 251–256.

14. *The Harvard Review,* Summer, 1963, Vol. I, No. 4, p. 33.

15. *Ibid.,* p. 34.

16. Gerome Ragni and James Rado, *Hair* (New York: Simon and Schuster, 1966), p. 41.

17. Jane Kramer, *Allen Ginsburg in America* (New York: Vintage Books, 1968–69), pp. 187–188.

18. "American Education as an Addictive Process and Its Cause," in Harold Jaffee and John Tytell (eds.), *The American Experience, A*

Radical Reader (New York, Evanston, London: Harper and Row, 1970), p. 202.

CHAPTER 2

1. See Albert Camus, *The Rebel*, translated by Anthony Bower (New York: Vintage, 1956), pp. 15, 22. Camus pervades the revolutionary ethos worldwide. See, for example, Carl Michaelson's report that he was the most widely read existentialist in Japan: *Japanese Contributions to Christian Theology* (Philadelphia: The Westminster Press, n.d.), p. 108.

2. *The Fall* (New York: Vintage, 1956), p. 97.

3. *The Plague* (New York: Modern Library, 1947), p. 278.

4. *The Stranger* (New York: Vintage, 1954), p. 151.

5. "A Kind Word for Conformity," *Saturday Review*, December 11, 1965, p. 24.

6. *The Rebel*, p. 2.

7. *Ibid.*, p. 13.

8. *Notebooks: 1935–1942*, translated and with preface and notes by Philip Thody (New York: Knopf, 1963), p. 54.

9. *The Fall*, pp. 132–133.

10. *Ibid.*, p. 133. *Cf.* James Baldwin, *The Fire Next Time* (New York: Dell Publishing Company, Inc., 1970), p. 120: ". . . I have met only a very few people—and most of these were not Americans—who had any real desire to be free. Freedom is hard to bear."

11. See John B. Cobb, Jr., *The Structure of Christian Existence* (Philadelphia: The Westminster Press, 1967), Chapter 5, "Axial Existence," pp. 52–59. Jaspers' views are contained in *The Origin and Goal of History* and are intended as a criticism of the Christian view of Christ as the center of history. One is reminded of Fulton Sheen's famous rhetoric that Jesus hit history with such impact that he broke it in two: B.C. and A.D. Jaspers denies and Cobb supports that rhetoric.

12. Isaiah 1: 4–21.

13. Harlow Shapley, *Of Stars and Men* (New York: The Washington Square Press, 1960), p. 57.

14. Jackson (ed.), *The Complete Works of the Rev. John Wesley* (Grand Rapids: Zondervan House, 1958–59), Vol. XI, p. 201. Reprint of 1872 edition.

15. Ingmar Bergman, *A Film Trilogy* (New York: The Orion Press, 1967), pp. 84–85. See Arthur Gibson, *The Silence of God* (New York, Evanston, and London: Harper and Row, 1969), p. 101. This is a

"creative response" to eight of Ingmar Bergman's films, including the famous trilogy on "God": *Through a Glass Darkly, Winter Light,* and *The Silence.*

16. *Ibid.*

17. Habakkuk 1: 1–4.

18. *Letters and Papers from Prison,* edited by Eberhard Bethge, translated by Reginald Fuller (New York: The Macmillan Company, 1962), p. 218, letter of July 16, 1944.

19. *Ibid.*

20. *Systematic Theology I* (Chicago: The University of Chicago Press, 1951), p. 205.

21. *Ibid.*

22. Marty and Peerman (eds.), *New Theology No. 1* (New York: The Macmillan Company, 1964), p. 151, article entitled "Nirvana and the Kingdom of God."

23. *Ibid.,* p. 153.

24. *The Gospel of Christian Atheism* (Philadelphia: The Westminster Press, 1966), p. 72.

25. *The Descent Into Hell* (Philadelphia and New York: J. B. Lippincott Company, 1970), p. 121.

CHAPTER 3

1. Chad Walsh, *Campus Gods on Trial* (New York: The Macmillan Company, 1962). See pp. 70–71.

2. The Complete Works of Friedrich Nietzsche, edited by Oscar Levy (London: George Allen and Unwin, 1910–1930), Vol. X, *Joyful Wisdom,* translated by Thomas Common, 1924, p. 167.

3. "Trash, Art and the Movies," *Harper's,* February, 1969, p. 81.

4. *The Thunder of Bare Feet,* pp. 31–32.

5. *Ibid.,* p. 32.

6. Quoted by John Hallowell, "The Free Society: Means or End?" *The Mission of the Christian College in the Modern World* (Washington, D.C.: The Council of Protestant Colleges and Universities, 1962), p. 90.

CHAPTER 4

1. (New York: Grove Press, Inc., 1966). Young's case in the first part of the book for "precise" expression in conjuring up copulation is absolutely devastating—the key witness for his case being an obscure Italian from the first half of the sixteenth century named Pietro Aretino.

In the second part, Young offers us a tight and persuasive analysis of the culpability of the "Church's" aversion to eros.

2. *Ibid.*, p. 173. Femina corpus opes animam vim lumina vocem Polluit adnihilat necat eripit orbat acerbat. Quoted in George Gordon Coulton, *Five Centuries of Religion* (Cambridge: Cambridge University Press, 1929), Vol. I, p. 177.

3. Baldwin, *The Fire Next Time*, p. 45. See Berman, *op. cit.*, pp. 104–109.

4. *Ibid.*, p. 61.

5. See *motive*, November, 1965, pp. 7–11, Hefner and Cox: "Sex: Myths and Realities." Cox's original reaction to Hefner can be found in *Christianity and Crisis*, April 17, 1961, reprinted in Wayne H. Cowan, *Witness to a Generation* (Indianapolis, New York, Kansas City: The Bobbs-Merrill Company, Inc., 1964), pp. 132–137.

6. *The Secular City*, new revised edition, p. 171.

7. Norman Mailer, *Why Are We in Vietnam?* (New York: G. P. Putnam's Sons, 1967), p. 109. Mailer's exorbitant indelicacy extrudes here and on pp. 110–111 to tie America's white pathology to our subliminal fear of flaccidity: "What if the Spades run away with the jewels?" (p. 110). "Spades" extrapolate to "women," "the Yellow races," "Africa," "adolescents," and "European nations." Even G-O-D (Mailer writes it G.O.D.—Grand Old Divinity) can't save us because "he" translates into the "biggest corporation of them all" (p. 111).

8. "No More Masterpieces," in Jaffee and Tytell, *op. cit.*, pp. 307–308.

9. *Ibid.*, p. 308.

10. Susan Sontag, *Against Interpretation* (New York: Dell Publishing Co., Inc., 1966), p. 165.

CHAPTER 5

1. Marty and Peerman, *New Theology No. 7* (London: The Macmillan Company, 1970), p. 102.

2. Günter Grass, *The Tin Drum* (Greenwich, Conn.: A Fawcett Crest Book, 1962), p. 268.

3. *Ibid.*

4. *Ibid.*, pp. 393–394.

5. See Immanuel Kant, *Critique of Judgment*, translated by J. H. Bernard (London: Macmillan, 1892), Introduction VII; Martin Heidegger, *Kant und das Problem der Metaphysik* (Bonn: Friedrich Cohens, 1929); and especially Herbert Marcuse, *Eros and Civiliza-*

tion, A Philosophical Inquiry into Freud (New York: Vintage Books, 1955), "The Aesthetic Dimension," pp. 157–179, particularly p. 161.

6. Ben Shahn, *The Shape of Content* (Cambridge: Harvard University Press, 1957), p. 3.

7. Ralph Stephenson and J. R. Debrix, *The Cinema as Art* (New York: Pelican, 1969), p. 19.

8. *Saturday Review,* December 28, 1968, p. 19.

9. Stephenson and Debrix, *op. cit.,* p. 36.

10. Quoted in Sidney Lanier, "Ingmar Bergman: Magician in the Cathedral," *Christianity and Crisis,* December, 1960, p. 199.

11. *Andover-Newton Quarterly,* November, 1962. This obscure journal was also my first introduction to Harvey Cox who contributed a flashy piece on contemporary cinema, revealing his long love affair with Fellini, climaxed several summers ago when he watched Fellini directing *Satyricon* outside Rome. Fellini asked Cox to step into a key character role for a moment of masterly contemplation—surely a juicy morsel for any feast of fools. Nothing came of that moment, except Cox's review of the movie in *Tempo* (most unfavorable!). I suppose Fellini's penchant for grotesque characters off the street gave Cox pause. His film reviews in *Tempo* and now *Christianity and Crisis* are alive with modish sense.

12. *Ibid.,* p. 23.

13. Alan McGlashan, *The Savage and Beautiful Country* (Boston: Houghton Mifflin Company, 1967), p. 47.

14. San Francisco *Chronicle,* June 5, 1967.

15. *Playboy,* XIII, September, 1966, p. 96. Also see *The Politics of Ecstasy* (New York: Putnam, 1968).

16. *The Doors of Perception and Heaven and Hell* (New York: Harper and Row, 1963), pp. 16–17.

17. *ETC,* December, 1965, p. 392.

18. "The Greening of America," *The New Yorker,* September 26, 1970, p. 111.

19. Larry McMurtry, *The Last Picture Show* (New York: Dell Publishing Co., Inc., 1966), p. 218.

20. John 1: 11–12.

CHAPTER 6

1. Albert Camus, *Noces* (Librairie Gallimard, 1950). See Camus' *Betwixt and Between* (1937) and *Nuptials* (1938), quoted in S. Beynon John, "Albert Camus," in Richard Kostelanetz (ed.), *On Contemporary Literature* (New York: Avon Books, 1964), p. 308.

2. Reprinted with permission from *motive* magazine, March 1962.

3. For another interesting Christmas play, with more intentionality, see Roszak, *op. cit.,* p. 39. There, the *same* December as Pacific's "pageant" (O axial time!), London's settlement house thirteen-year-olds had Santa imprisoned by immigrant authorities (no permission to enter England) and released by an "exotic species of being" known as "hippies," accompanied by shiva dancing, strobe lights, and jangling sitars.

4. Malcolm Boyd, *As I Live and Breathe, Stages of an Autobiography* (New York: Random House, 1969), p. 213.

5. See *An Alternative Future for America,* Essays and Speeches of Robert Theobald, edited by Kendall College (Chicago: The Swallow Press, 1968). *Cf.* Fuller in *Utopia or Oblivion: The Prospects for Humanity* (New York: Bantam Books, 1969) where he makes an amazing prediction that there is a "new man" being raised up at this very moment of the "collapse" of the Western tradition. He is a man who is finding the "human" use of space through technological imagination. And the matrix for this "new man" is precisely located as the Bay Area in California! (Berkeley, San Francisco, and San Jose). Stockton, unhappily, is just outside the perimeter of this technocratic eschaton—still a "nowhere place." So it goes. I think the final honor for the "new man" will probably go to the Chinese, not the Californians (see Herbert Read, *The Redemption of the Robot* [New York: Trident Press, 1966], pp. 188–199, and any random remarks by Robert Scheer, former editor of *Ramparts,* on his recent three-month visit to the People's Republic of China). As a matter of fact, see Richard Nixon!

6. Norman O. Brown, *Life Against Death* (Middletown, Conn.: Wesleyan Univ. Press, 1959), pp. 32–33; also pp. 307–322.

7. Read, *The Redemption of the Robot,* pp. 202–203.

8. *On the Aesthetic Education of Man,* translated by Reginald Snell (New Haven: Yale University Press, 1954), p. 134; cited in Read, *op. cit.,* p. 204.

9. *Ibid.,* p. 137; Read, *op. cit.,* pp. 204–205.

10. From a paper read at the American Academy of Religion, October 24, 1969, at Boston, Massachusetts, entitled "Eschatological Nudity: Body, Soul, and the New Sensibility." The remarkable phrase "eschatological nudism" appears in Mircea Eliade, *The Two and the One* (New York and Evanston: Harper and Row, 1965), p. 125, in connection with a strange cult appearing on the island of Espiritu Santo, one of the New Hebrides, in the years 1944–1945. This nudist cult destroyed their clothes and ornaments, lived completely communally and openly —performing even the sexual acts publicly and in the daylight, after

"the fashion of dogs and birds" (p. 126). The leader, one Tsek, thought he was establishing "Paradise on Earth": "Men will no longer work; they will have no more need for tools, domestic animals or possessions. Once the old order is abolished the laws, rules, and taboos will lose their reason. The prohibitions and customs sanctioned by tradition will give place to absolute liberty; in the first place to sexual liberty, to orgy. For, in human society, it is sexual life that is subject to the strictest taboos and constraints. To be free from laws, prohibitions and customs, is to rediscover primordial liberty and blessedness, the state which preceded the present human condition . . ." (p. 127). The nudists also waited for some mythical group called "The Americans" (!) to come and bring them great gifts of food and usher in the era of plenty—the Americans being the last group of whites with which the natives had come in contact during the Second World War. Eliade comments that the early enthusiasm of the movement has now been replaced with "discouragement and lassitude." The Americans never arrived of course, perhaps detained by problems at home fomented by their own sexual-freedom, anarchic, no-work, nudist cults. Tsek, thy name is legion!

CONCLUSION

1. *Love, Power, and Justice* (New York: Oxford Press, 1954), p. 72.
2. *Ibid.*, p. 77.
3. *Radical Monotheism and Western Culture* (New York: Harper and Bros., 1960), p. 37.
4. *Ibid.*, p. 25.
5. *Ibid.*, p. 32.